I WILL NOT _____ **.

(**I will not... let you encourage me to doubt myself.)
(**I will not ... fear the unknown.)
(**I will not... deny my dreams.)
... there are endless possibilities
All subjective, yet all pertinent to how we perceive and live our lives...

- denise felice

About the author: Denise Felice, an international freelance photographer, holds a Bachelors' of Fine Art in graphic design and photography. She is also a visiting educator, in the United States and the United Kingdom, for prevention programs encouraging tolerance and problem solving. Her photographic images and insightful writing provoke an emotional inhale, possibly a sense of peace and understanding from within. We hope that they too will affect you in this way as you now join us for a sense of calm, even for a very brief moment, during our busy lives.

(an accompanying teacher's guide is available upon request at eedenisee@aol.com)

Balboa Press books may be ordered through booksellers or by contacting:

Balboa Press
A Division of Hay House
1663 Liberty Drive
Bloomington, IN 47403
www.balboapress.com
1-(877) 407-4847

LIBRARY OF CONGRESS CATALOGING-IN-PUBLICATION DATA
Felice, Denise.
I WILL NOT _____**. / by denise felice.   p. cm

Summary: Intrinsic images with journal passages bring the reader to a deep level of introspection and connection with life and living. Although we all belong to humanity & to this international world of 'community', isolation is a universal detriment of being human, When a person is weakened & their motivation has expired this is when we must open our hearts and reach out to others... because we understand their sorrow, we know the hidden secrets of these deep feelings of despair, & AND their innermost wish to regain hope.
1. Angels-Fiction   2. Poetry-Fiction   3. Relationships-Fiction   I. Title.

Cover and book design by Denise Felice
'An Alternative Reality', page 4, by Stephen J. Booker
'Angelic Greetings', page 66, by Alexander Buchan
'I've visited a place I've never been', page 67, by Stephen J. Booker

ISBN: 978-1-4525-3532-6 (sc)

Library of Congress Control Number: 2011909325

Printed in the United States of America

Balboa Press rev. date: 8/31/2011

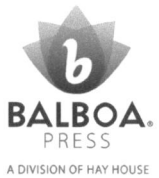

BALBOA.
PRESS
A DIVISION OF HAY HOUSE

TITLE: "I WILL NOT _____ **."
Writing & Art Work by Author, denise felice

DEDICATION

april, connie, dana, erin, & karen

 you are my life's blood and breath, you are and always will be part of my heart and loves of my life forever. thank you for being what 'true family' is fantasized about... yes, Unconditional Love in its true rarest form, meaning occurring in reality xxxx love forever, denise/mom

IN APPRECIATION

nataline aron, steve booker, alex buchan, aj carter, ann cripps, sue heller, marlene karas, christine kilger, & janet wearmouth Also my three lynn university angels of a fortunate lifetime: sue merrill, mary reid, & marlene turner

 In appreciation always to you my dearest friends, you have given needed momentum and hope to my photography & inner voice on a daily basis.

All of you gathered around Alex's angel have made this book possible. The world and my life are truly blessed by having you, my friends, as part of me. Many of like minds & kind hearts gather together not only to discuss peace but to CREATE peace in our lives and our world... let's enter the happiest of New Years with full unselfish desire and enthusiastic certainty for world peace. Thank you for your loving & heartfelt guidance & strength... I will treasure you always, much love, denise

DEAR READERS

I apologize if I sound pretentious or judgmental, this of course is not my intention, nor is it to sound ludicrous or incomprehensible :) The Title of this book is interchangeable for each person to put in their own applicable/emotional statement. "Titles" are also interchangeable during the different periods of our lives.

I hope you feel comfortable enough to be of open mind and heart... to include your own thoughts and interplay with my images in writing> please write on each page of this book to make it your own personal tool for expression and of life xoxoxxo

Thank you for your time and interest; I truly appreciate your visit and accompaniment along this journey through my images & writing, ...to create an understanding that we are all of Humanity and we should never feel alone...

An Alternative Reality

-Stephen John Booker

1.   I look out my window
And what do I see
A vast expanse
Known as eternity

Of course alternatively
I might more locally see
The short cut grass
And an occasional tree

A view encountered in its expanse
arrived at by no casual chance
For in the depths of the mind
we decide what the eye will find

It would be fair to say
That on any given day
The view we perceive
We could take or leave

But there is an exception
To that general perception
The chemical trigger
That injects a new vigour

2.   I look out my window
And what do I see
A radiance of colour
And untold opportunity

It can brighten what's dull
add rainbows of colour
Make what's deflated
so much fuller

Replaces an ember with a fire
Turning lethargy into desire
Reverse a feeling of what's less,
causing what's flat to effervesce

Confidence will fly,
up to a new high
The self esteem we seek
at its ultimate peak

Be cautious and think: We could be mistaken?
To consider old feelings all forsaken
To mistake this temporary, psychological shift
as permanent and lasting; yet an illusionary lift

3.   I look out my window
And what do I see
My very own version
of what's reality

FOREWORD

-LOTFAÏ, Artistic Director & Designer,
CHEZ LOTFAÏ Film & Television Production Agency, Paris

My daughter is now 2 years. She is the most beautiful person of my world. Her innocence reminds me how we were, before we were 'told' to change while growing up : change because of the media… because of what politics in many ways do with our lives. We have 2 choices : to accept or to learn to stay true to ourselves. I never accepted as a fatality the powerful politics, racist propaganda, or television news I was exposed to; 'they' are not ones to decide what we must choose to see or should believe. Why should media 'hype' decide for you what's 'in', how you should be dressed or who You should be?... Freedom is what I want to offer to my daughter : the right of Free-Will. I also offer the right to be respectful. Last time, she came back from the day-nursery with a small band-aid on her hand. She showed it to me and told me a little girl had bit her. I sat her on my knee and asked her to listen to me. I told her "when someone does something wrong to you, even if he/she bites you or hits you, don't try the revenge. It will never bring you something positive. Be sorry for this person, because if you do bad things to someone you do bad things to yourself."... I'm not sure if she understood every word I said, but I know the message was and is clear, and I will bring this truth to her all my life.

... I believe the most important thing is 'our personal goals'... We can make people happy in many ways, yet we must find our own ways to do that. Especially for persons like us, who are artists and who need to fulfill themselves... never be frustrated, never put things we love aside (like writing books, directing, shooting, writing scripts... in 1 word : Creating). We need to find and stay in our paths... without it, we are completely lost... when we are lost we make mistakes with people who surround us because we are not happy with our own universe. That's what I feel... I mean that's what I felt... I was lost... We have to look for an echo of our spirits in the greatest men and women in our history….Martin Luther King Jr., Gandhi…
That's how we can find the way back our "US"... our "I"... our "ME". Believe me Denise, I've never been so aware of what I want to do with my life now : spreading respect, love, happiness and more and more good energies around me and… Something very important also : never forget my goals and lose myself. .. I know you can relate to this. THIS LETTER WILL PROBABLY FIND YOU IN YOUR MORNING, SO HAVE A NICE DAY FULL OF LOVE, PEACE AND CREATIVITY.- LOTFAÏ

"I never had the joy to hear a story from my mom's voice, nor my dad's, when I was a little boy ready to fall into my dreams. And the only way for me to be a dragon hunter was in the pictures stuck on my bedroom's walls. I used to randomly take one picture, and let the magic begin.

This is exactly what I've found in the art of Denise. The story she's telling you is yours. Every time you find a picture Denise took, you are this pirate who just found a treasure : you preciously keep it.

Having the chance to discover all these magic moments in one book makes me realize that we are now able to share these stories to the ones we love.

How the pirates we were, can now begin to share…" Lotfai

my psychobabble to you with a hug from my heart

-denise felice

YOUR perspective on interpersonal dynamics molds your individuality. Confidence in life begins with choices and also with trusting ourselves to know that personal direction is always a choice...

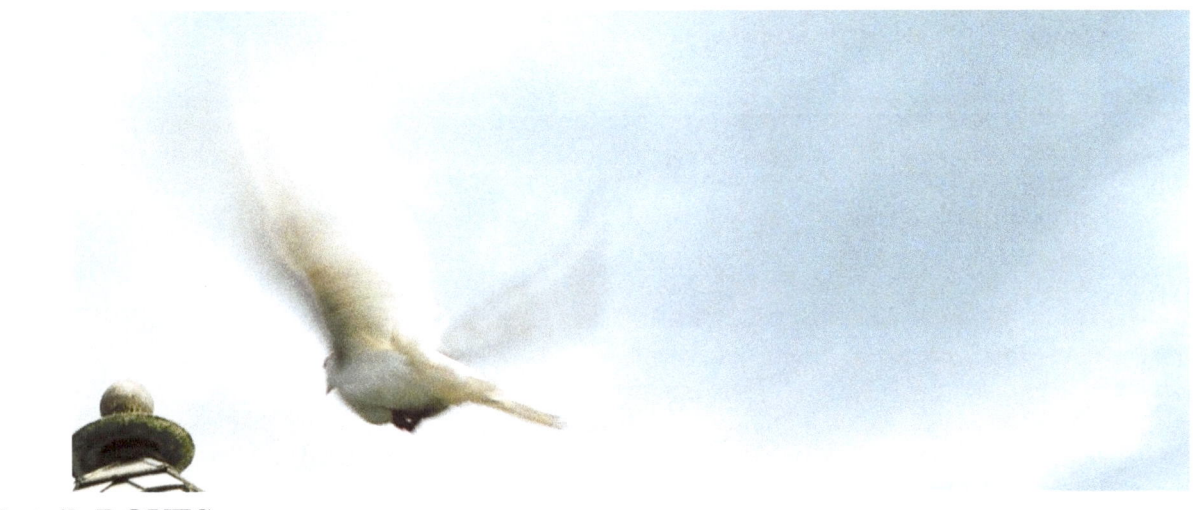

Detail: DOVES

Thanks for the kind words & confidence spoken about my art, it is so true about having a dream to become a wonderful reality, one which I pursue in my heart yet not as actively as I should in the professional realm... acknowledging & affirming: procrastination in one's own matters is the easiest thing to accomplish because then no one will be disappointed except oneself ... I guess it is like this in all areas of life. One should just feel content with their actual activity of creation & then let go so fear cannot paralyze. Thank you my wonderful friends, you have lifted my spirit, much love!

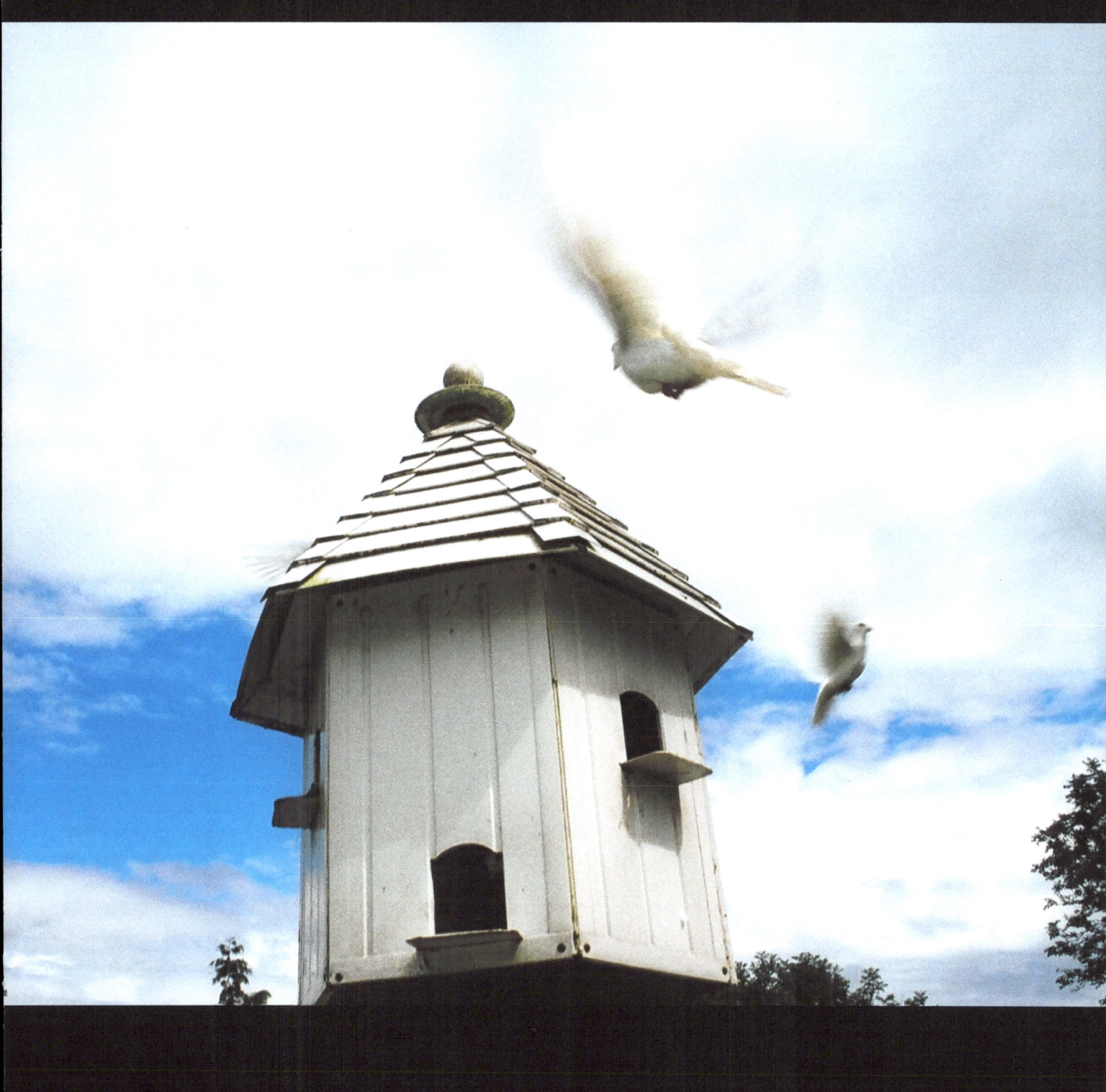

Necessity is the mother of re-invention. Can you open up to yourself & acknowledge who you are?> wants, desires, needed forgiveness, secrets?

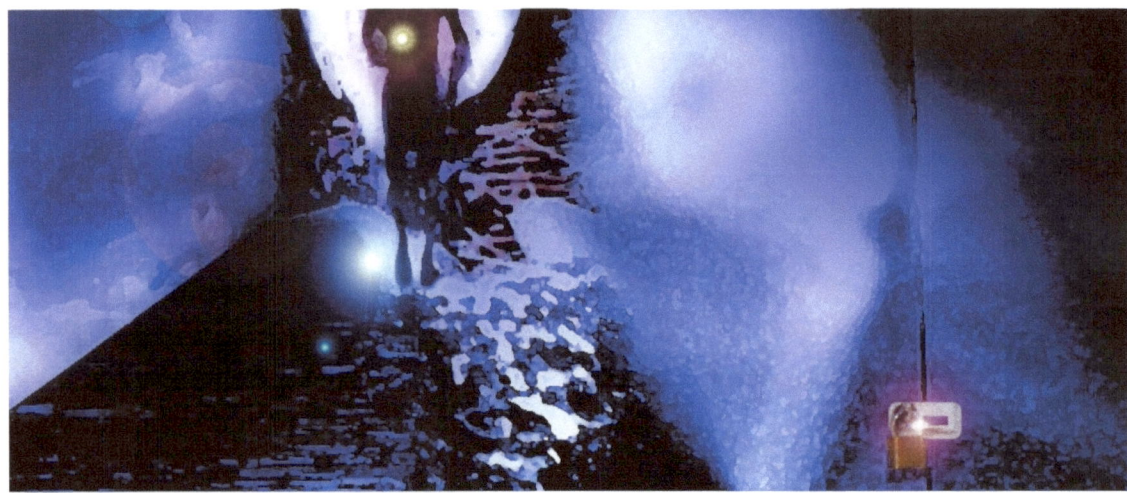

Detail: RESCUE FROM DARKNESS

Planting a seed of confidence deep inside to reach the goals you really desire and deserve... As you know life is very short, happiness is hard to come by, especially if we have to keep picking up the pieces for people that keep breaking things; lots of love always to you my friend/ may a new ability to focus on happiness develop into way of living!> energize and concentrate on the good things already present in your life so they won't wilt... xoxoxo

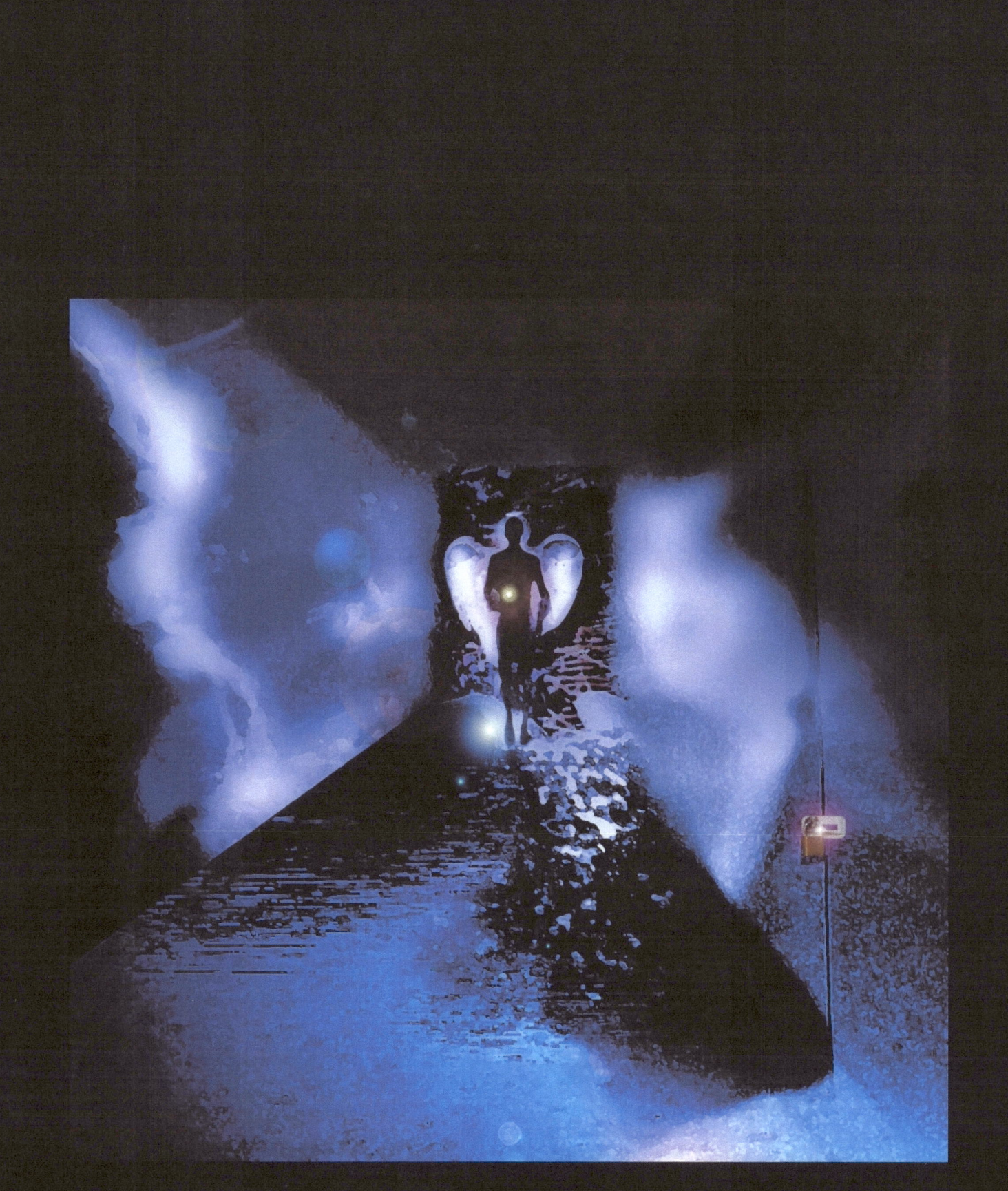

Happiness is uncontrived & can be reached when our natural instinctual need to be oneself is accepted in our functional environment.

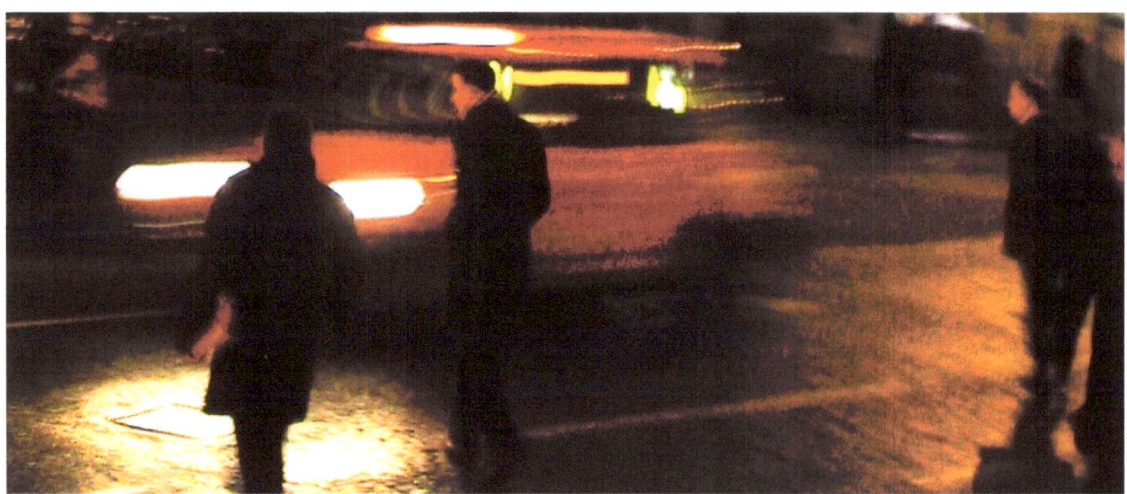

Detail: LONDON LOOK

It was fun laughing with you on the phone last pm, weird placement of us yes, & I was still on UK time!… also about midnight magic, thanks to you & the walk up the hill in the rain last year now New Years has a memory :) no regrets, only smiles! Last night was ok here… just another function, I snuck out a little after the Times-Square ball drop (talk about traditions since childhood!). Glad to hear you're again with people that know you as you, and they are part of your life; I believe this shall be an interesting year :) many wishes for a great, not only start of a year, but a full year of good things!

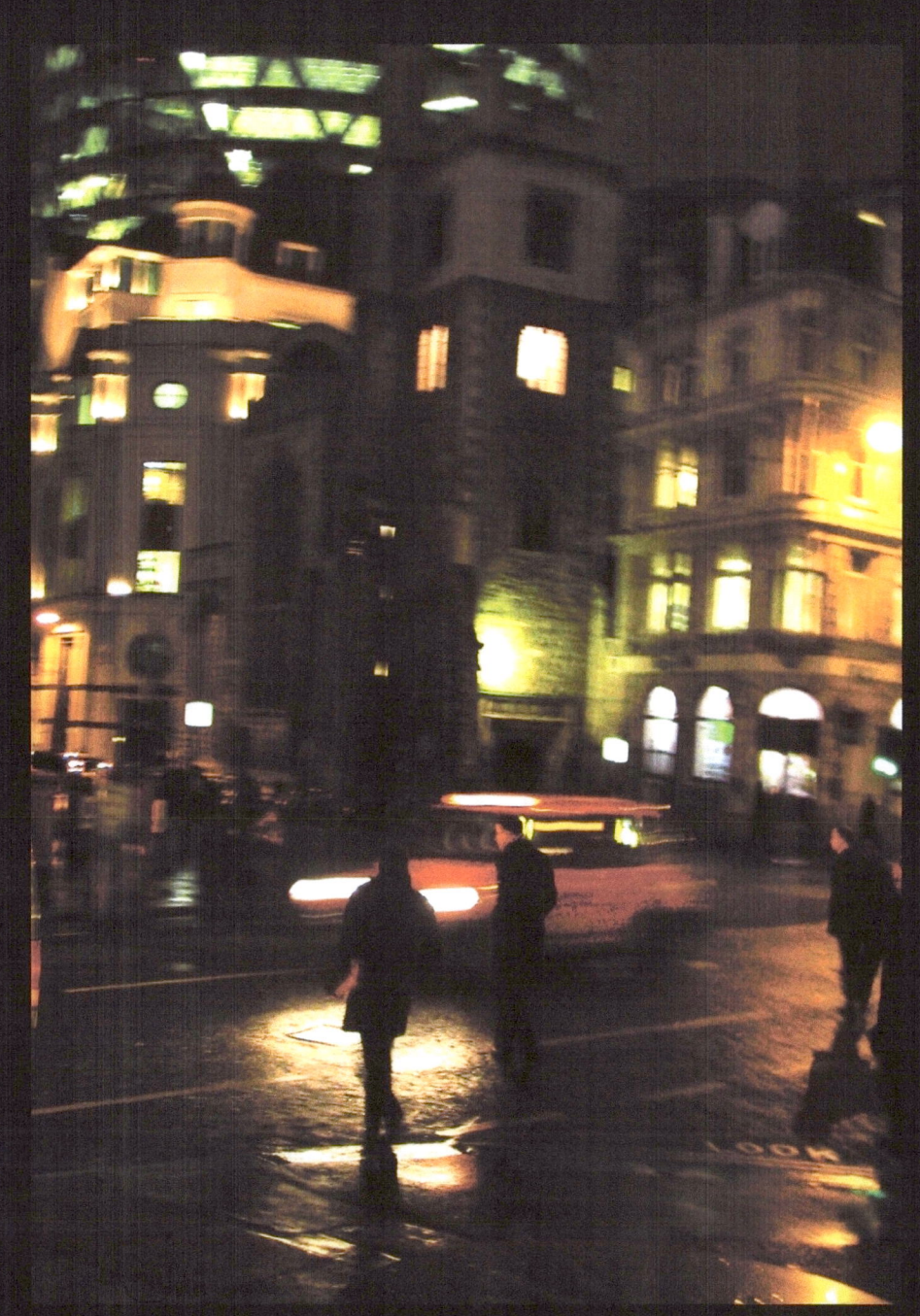

Quest first for internal happiness & contentment, then the physical environment of happiness has a better chance to happen. Don't over-think, discover what makes you unique & special... add in reflection, sensitivity & kindness to others... & of course FUN: I've found adventures can be many fold, from exploring one's mind to photographing in the highlands!

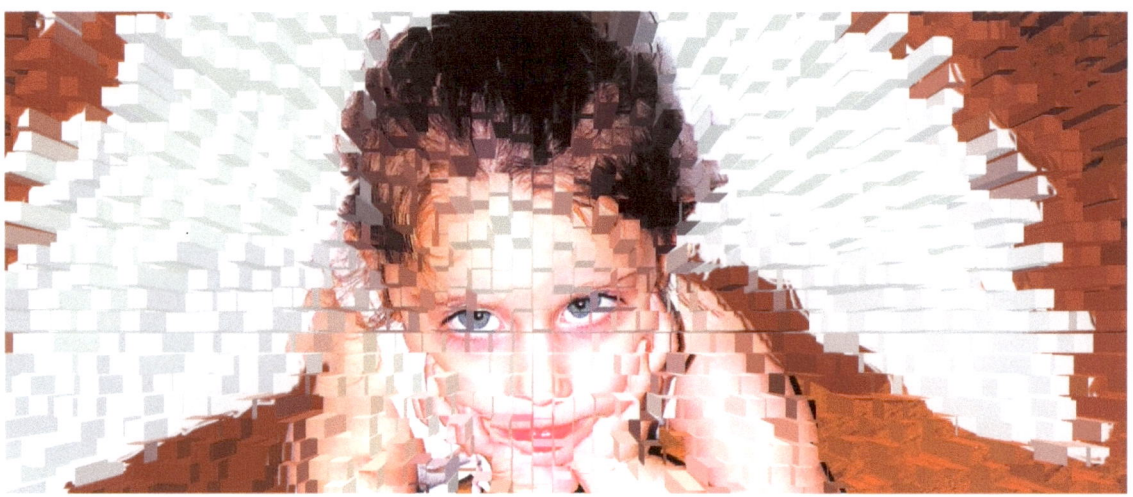

Detail: CITY GUARDIAN

The quest for happiness becomes a journey of renewal and no longer a want for happiness, because joy is a constant internal element thanks to knowing what life has to offer and the VALUE of being here ALIVE. The ability to creatively express, to be genuine... Knowing I can make a difference by helping others are all attainable goals because, you, my teachers have helped me believe in myself.

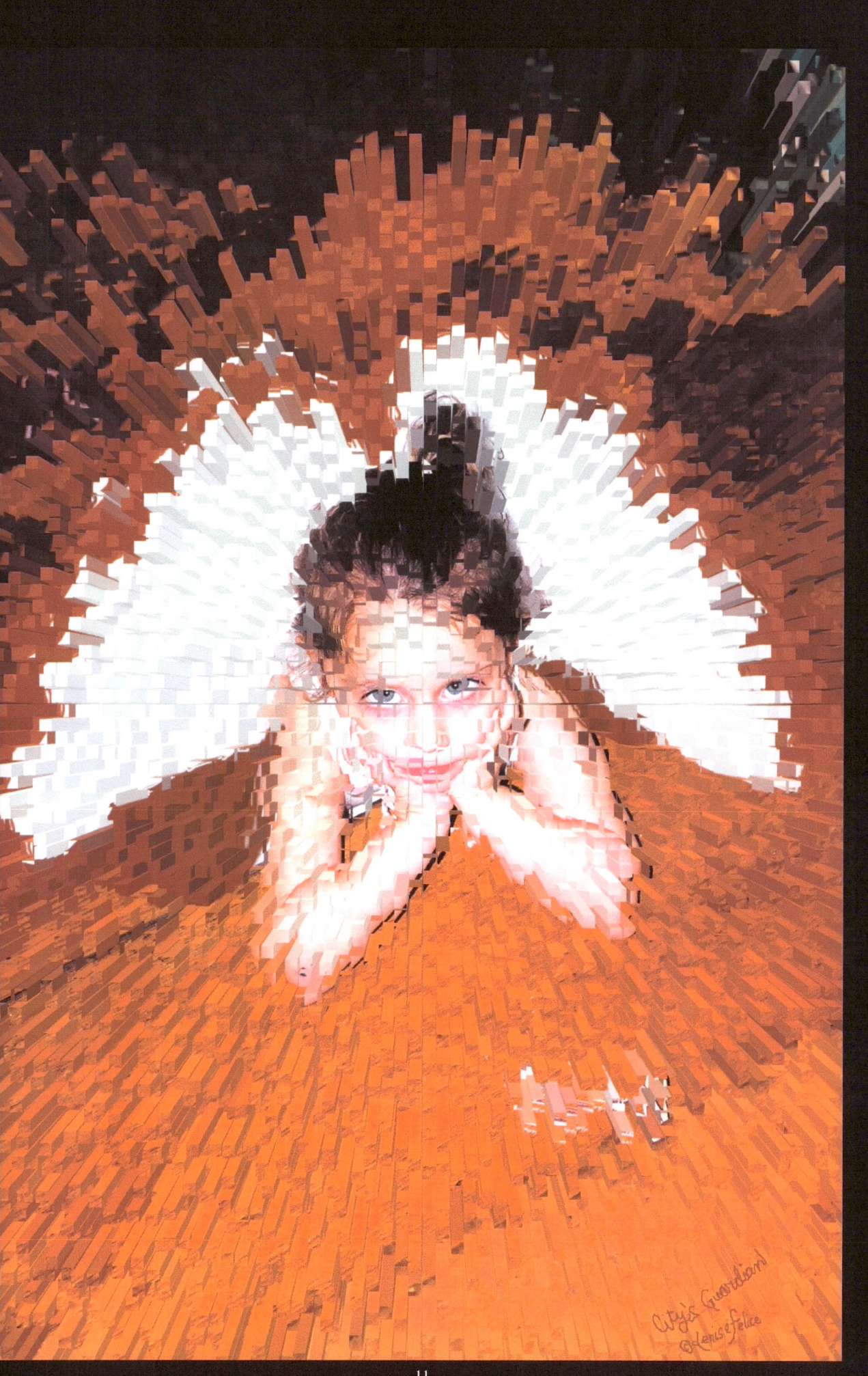

Comfort heals even for the seemingly impenetrable or needless (I am human also). Life is a journey & there will be sincere people walking the path beside us. Question only connections that are doing harm, and accept kind words from the many others as inspiration and a reflection of your own kindness...

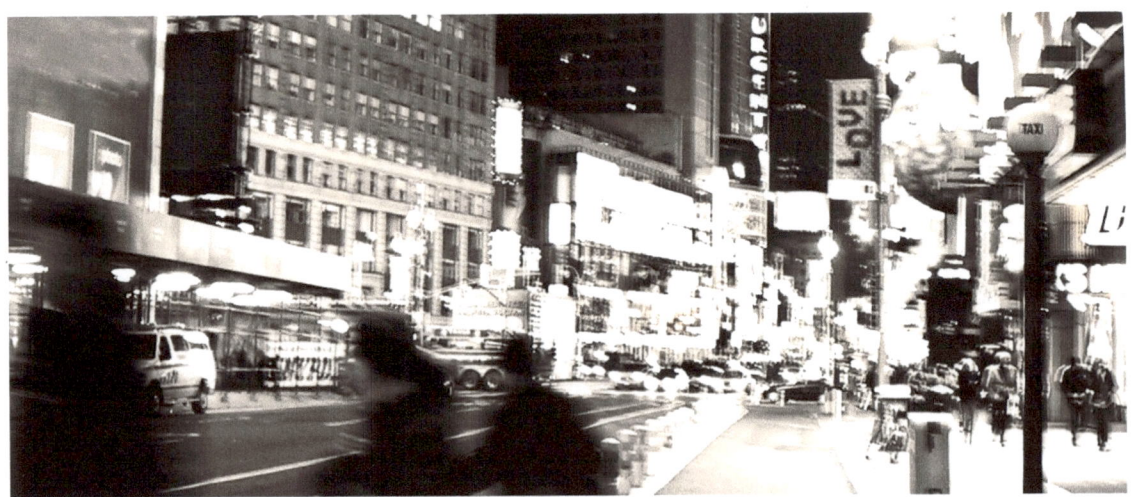

Detail: NYC URGENT LOVE

...sometimes out of our hands, possibly the capacity for one (me) to understand at times or failure to recognize or acknowledge> the recognition of the strength of our inner soul, man may call as psyche, helps with peace & understanding about life. I share your values about the interplay of relationships; life is so precious to each & every person. Intimate partners could be a natural comfort & joy (also a refuge to calm inner uneasiness) to each other, rather than be the cause of strife or needed explanation or justification of oneself... guess it goes back to unconditional love & a natural acceptance of one another as a total person.

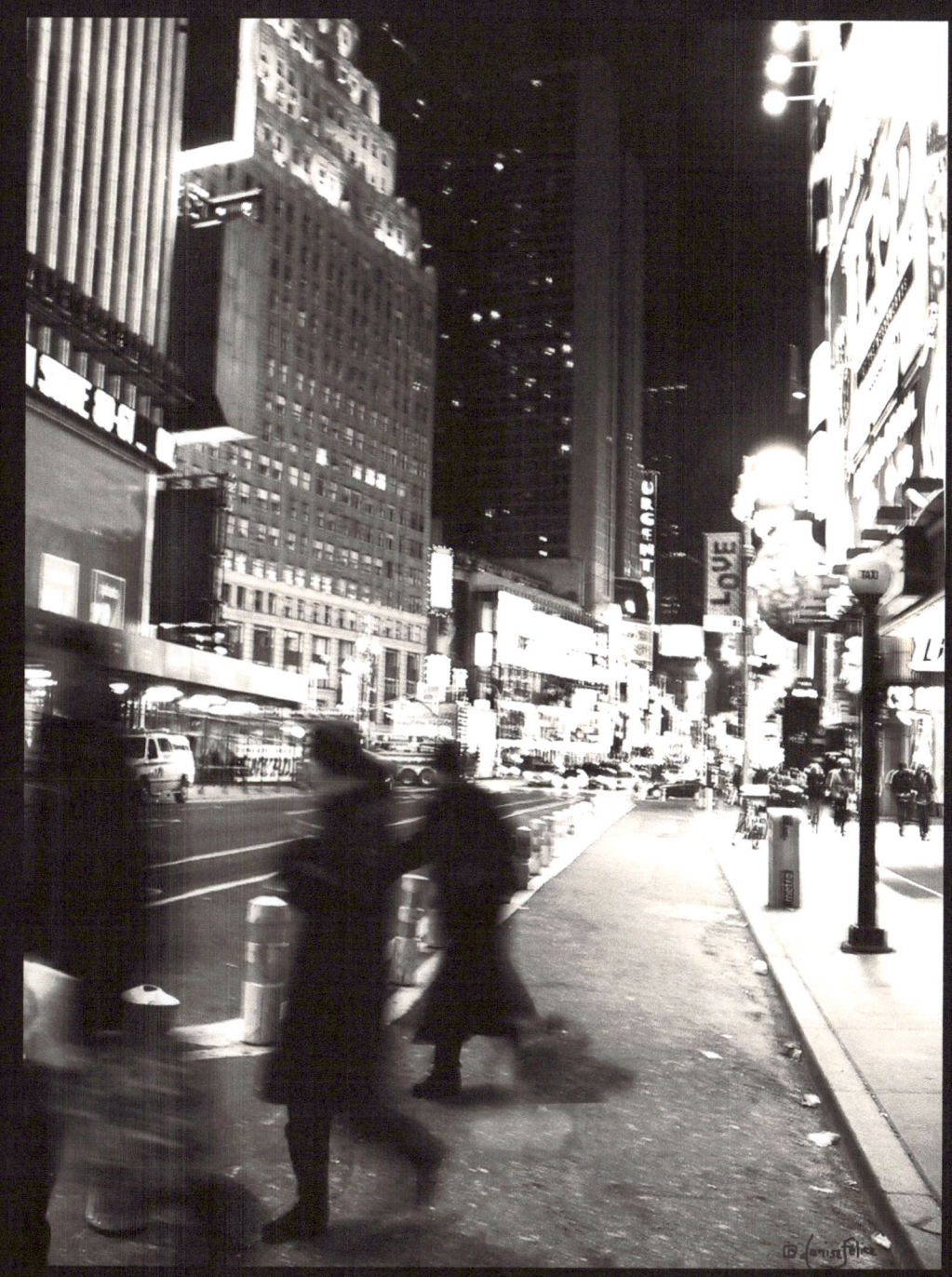

Poor communication is only an excuse for non-caring. Everyone wants to feel cared about & understood, but then some begin to take these gifts of human connection for granted.

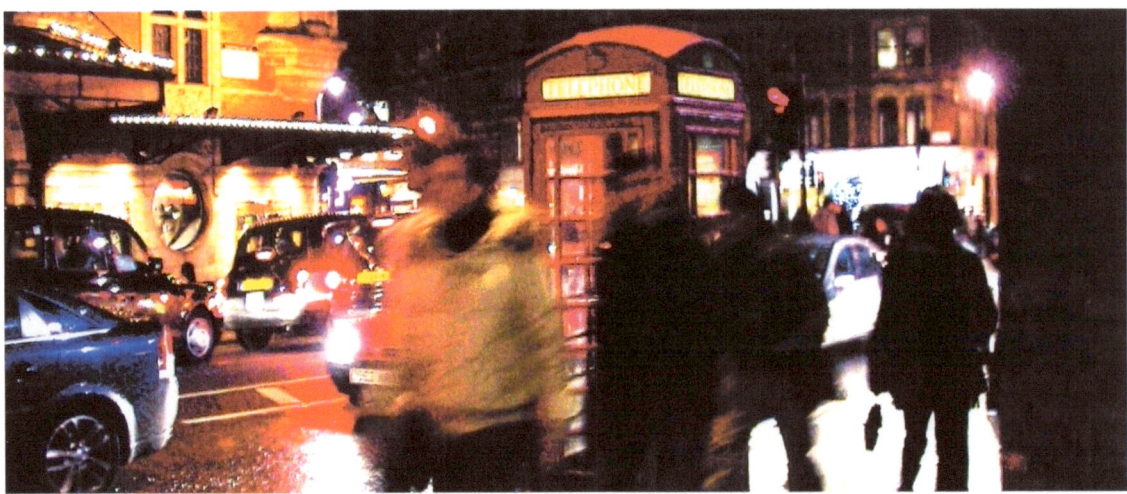

Detail: DISCONNECTED

Why do you love me, yet not pay attention to me or protect me from your hurt onto me? Challenges, integrity, you have 2 personalities and points of soul, I was in love with the first man I knew. Excuses of distance, difficulty, & time are just that excuses. We know when you truly want something you go full-out without hesitation to attain it. I miss experiencing life with you xxxo

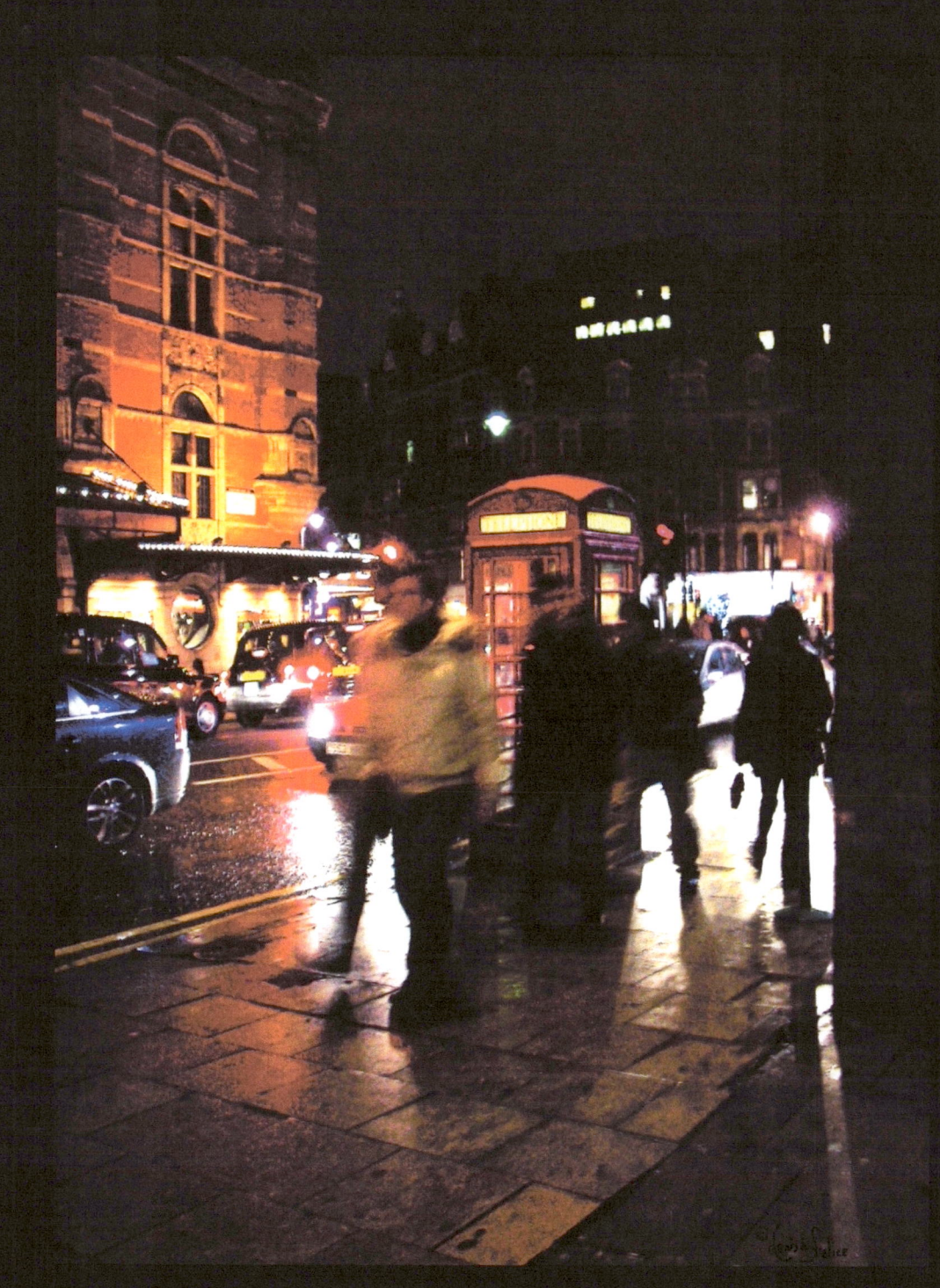

Prepare a strong foundation for flexibility & the ability for adaptation. Getting through rough times can create a brand new day which may only be visible & understandable once the dust has cleared.

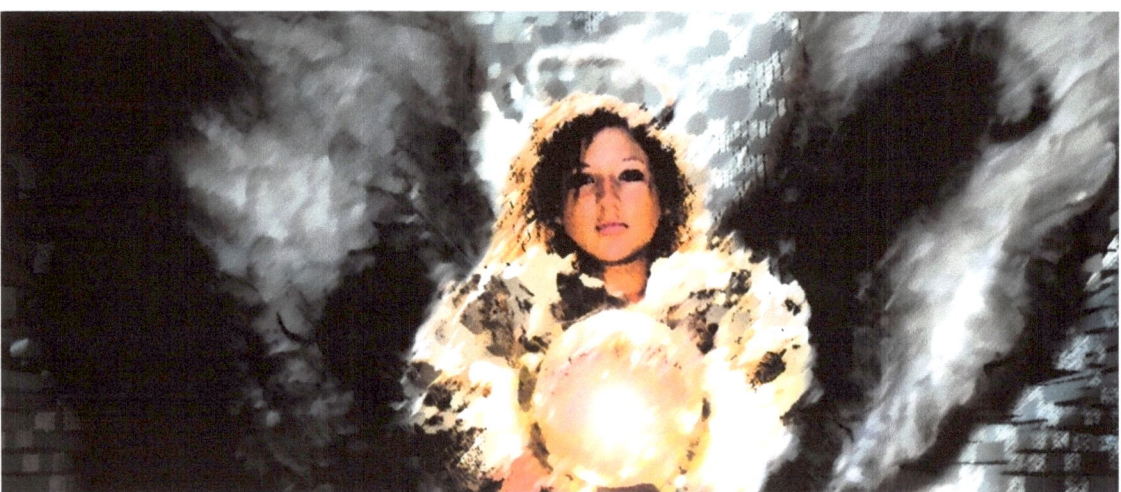

Detail: STRENGTH

;) life>not> la la la :) ….. find where you have control of each factor & do the torture of change. You are worth your own attention, you give it to everyone else. Call me later if you want someone to breathe with. Shit will dry & flake away after a while… yes, change is possible. The 'quality' of understanding reasons of why we go through seasons of storms may not be apparent, yet we have no choice but to look with our hearts to the future while protecting our eyes from present damage. Storms are finite, false visions of permanence can unfairly keep the future in darkness, even when the storm has past. Maybe I am speaking of forgiveness, I am not sure 'cuz it is late & I am tired…

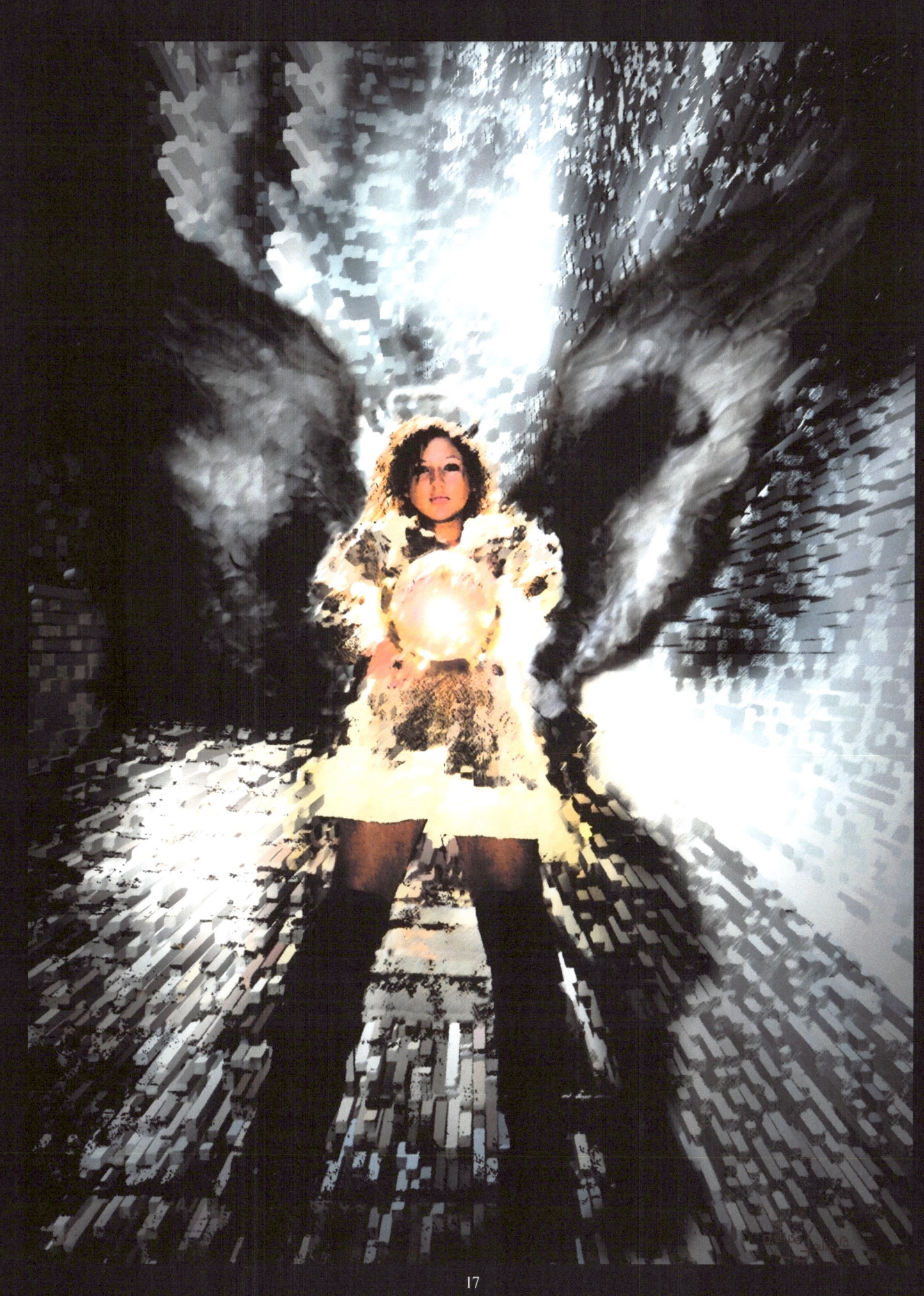

Create good, it will multiply and return many times back to you in this close & closed circle of life! Find special role models in life whom teach by example, to treat each & every person with dignity & omniscient understanding.

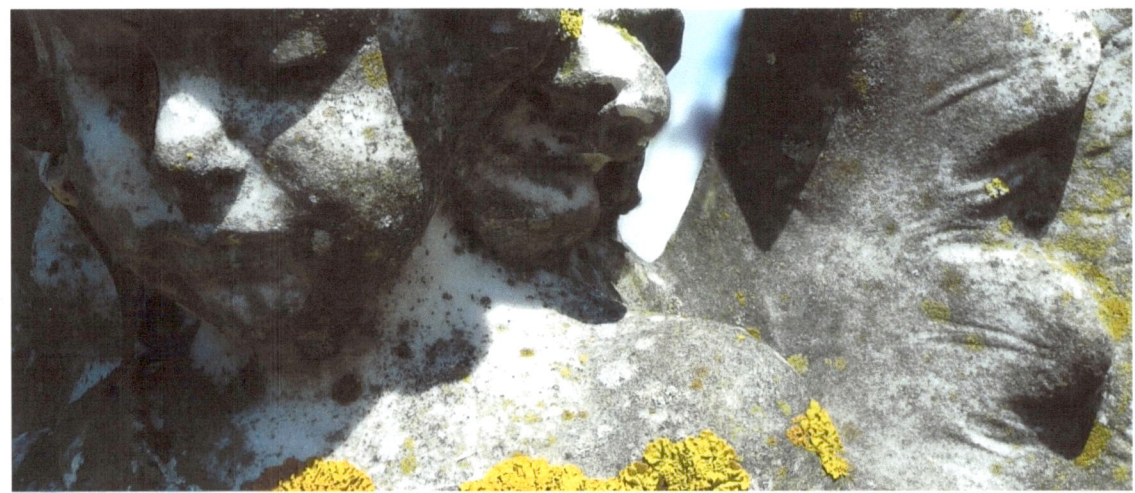

Detail: ANGEL OF HOPE & UNDERSTANDING

Love is much more than just a physical connection between a man & a woman. Ultimate love= Unconditional love: 'as to put one before one-self'. Not many people are capable of unconditional love. Stemming from internal compassion, the ability to understand others and give care that is void of any need for personal gain. When this is only one sided, even in marriage or with parent-child relationships, the blindness and/or inability to love and nurture a person equally causes relationships to falter…

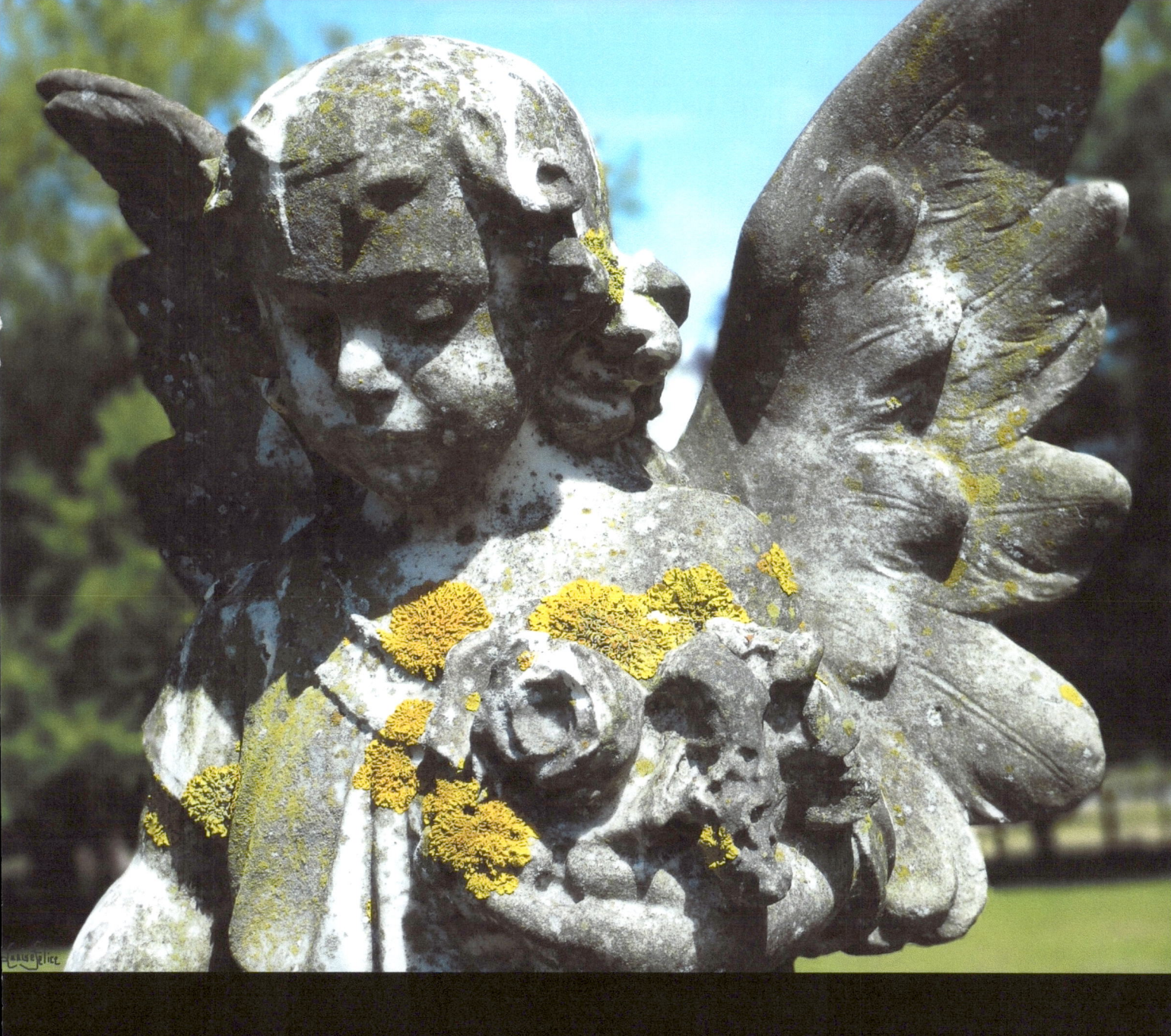

We must "trust by truth, not by words or selected actions". Wouldn't it be great if truth could prevail at all times, not trust> trust is an element that implies that one is acting in a particular way to please a person. Truth on the other hand transcends into more than mere words can describe.

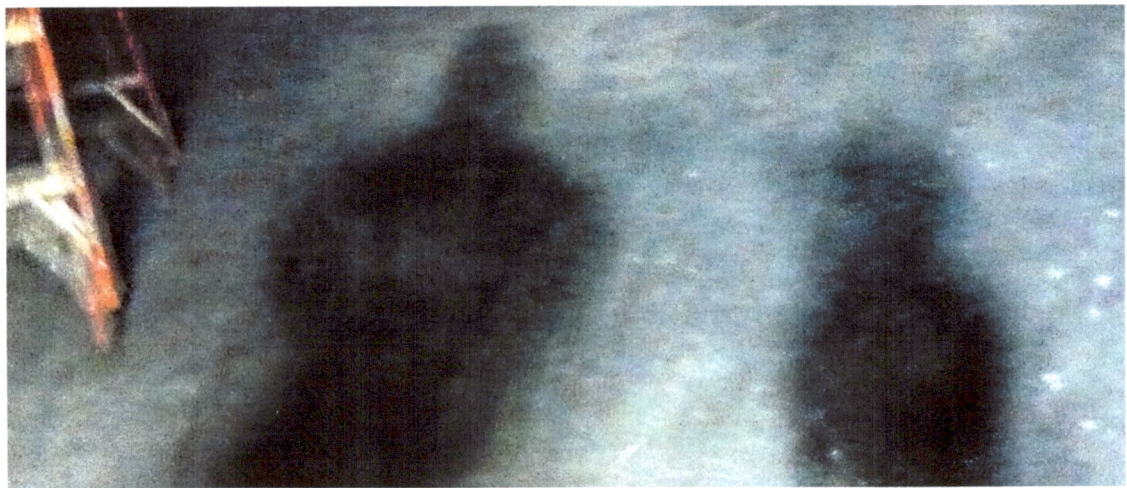

Detail: TRUTH HAS NOT A SHADOW

It would have to be truth in all areas of communication & relationship: truth is openness/ it gives respect & shows value towards your mate. It gives the couple the opportunity to assess situations, to make clear decisions, & it also prevents so many of the pitfalls of relationship breakdown. Fear & Silence do not protect a relationship, they instead spark jealousy, paranoia, double-guessing, and denial of dreams/desires> such factors which create more dismay and distance between 2 people.

"trust by truth, not by words or selected actions"

A muse comes from within oneself; the muse = inner creativity… desire & also discontent / expressed via your self expression & voice via your art = YOU!

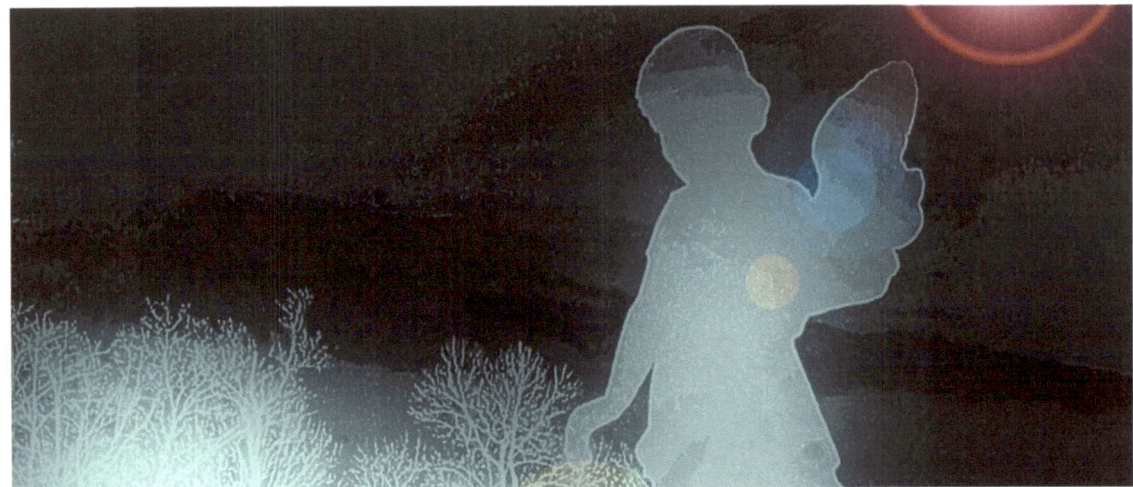

Detail: LIFE'S JOURNEY

I am sitting here eating spinach leaves (since the chocolate has vanished hours ago) & drinking coke from the bottle, as a writer would smoke his pipe and scratch his forehead… creativity is a thread that has been constant & important throughout my life; have you ever been so involved with a "project" you then just flow with a muse, losing track of time or even caring about time?… You my friend are such a talented writer & editor> BRAVO! YOU are an INSPIRATION!!

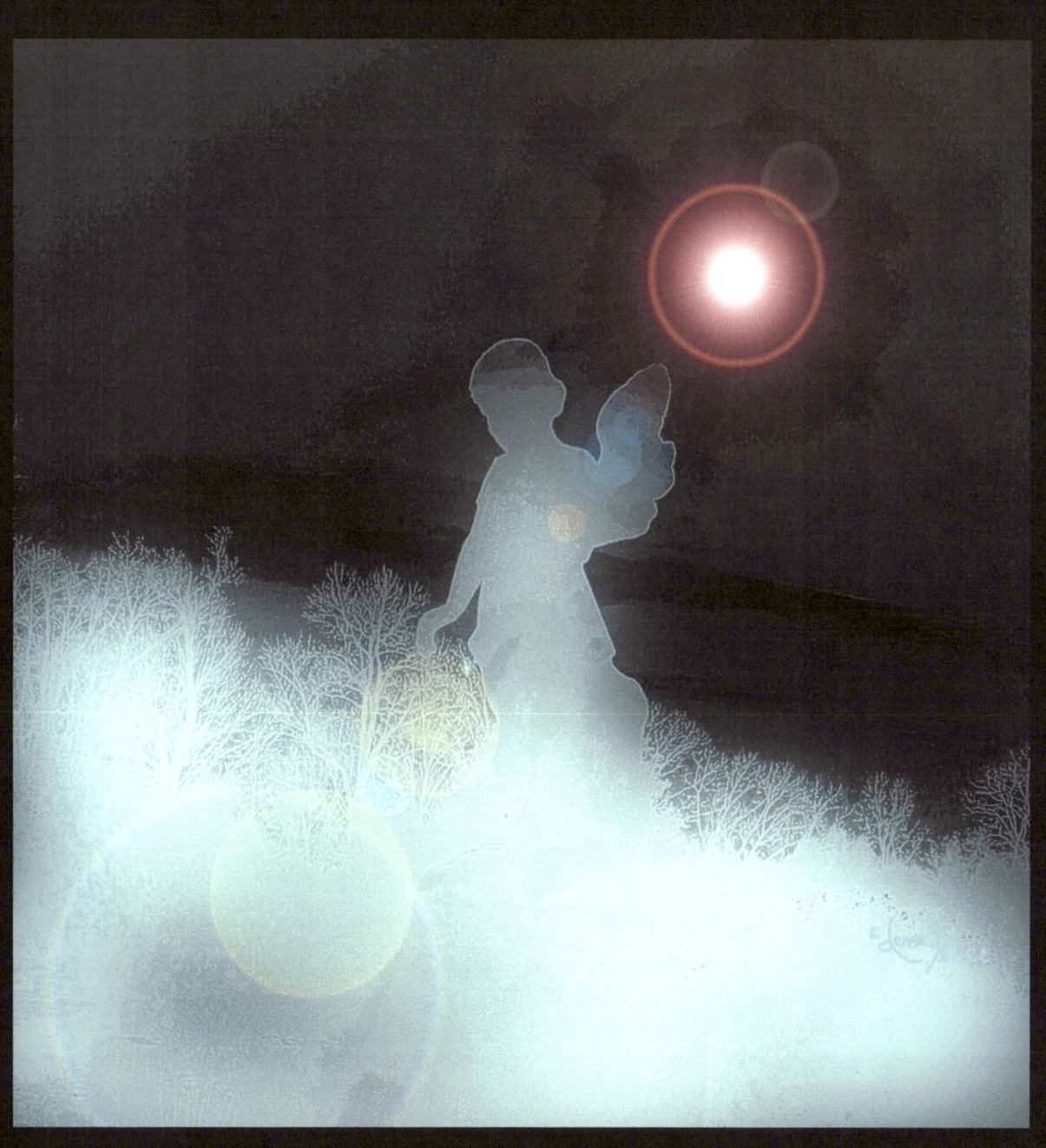

You are not insane; you are actually in the middle of insanity. The monkey in the middle never reaches the unnecessary ball which creates unnecessary want. This ball being thrown nigh close to grasp yet never attainable> thank goodness you cannot reach it, it may have exploded right in your hands and smeared over your eyes down onto your heart.

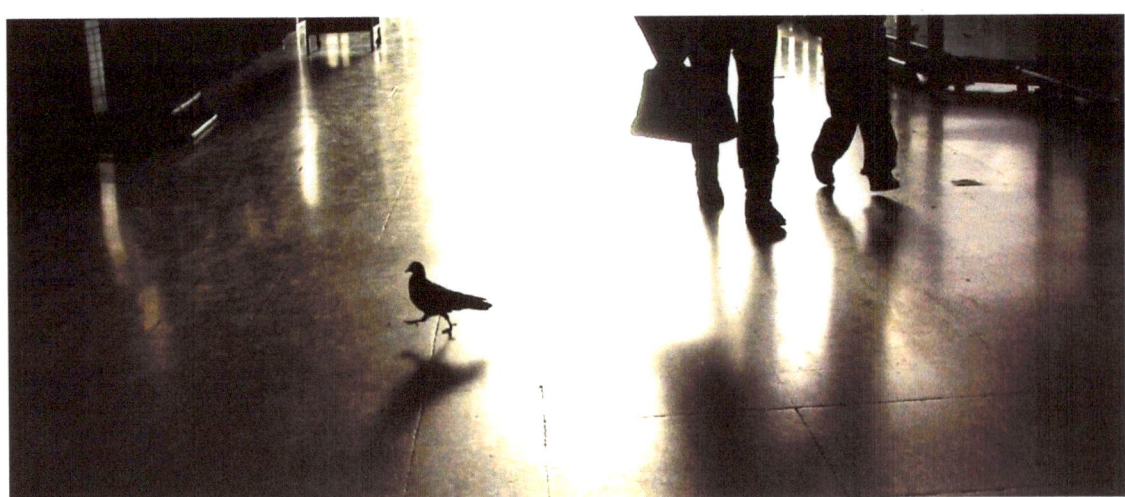

Detail: VICTORIA STATION

xoxo thanks for the love, no worries nothing is drastic, just thinking of all my wasted energy of false direction, death of motivation...completion of brainless tasks we all have to do ultimately blocks our creativity & growth> hence a vicious circle and never a true direction or decision, lol!!!... = i gave up... which might be a good thing??

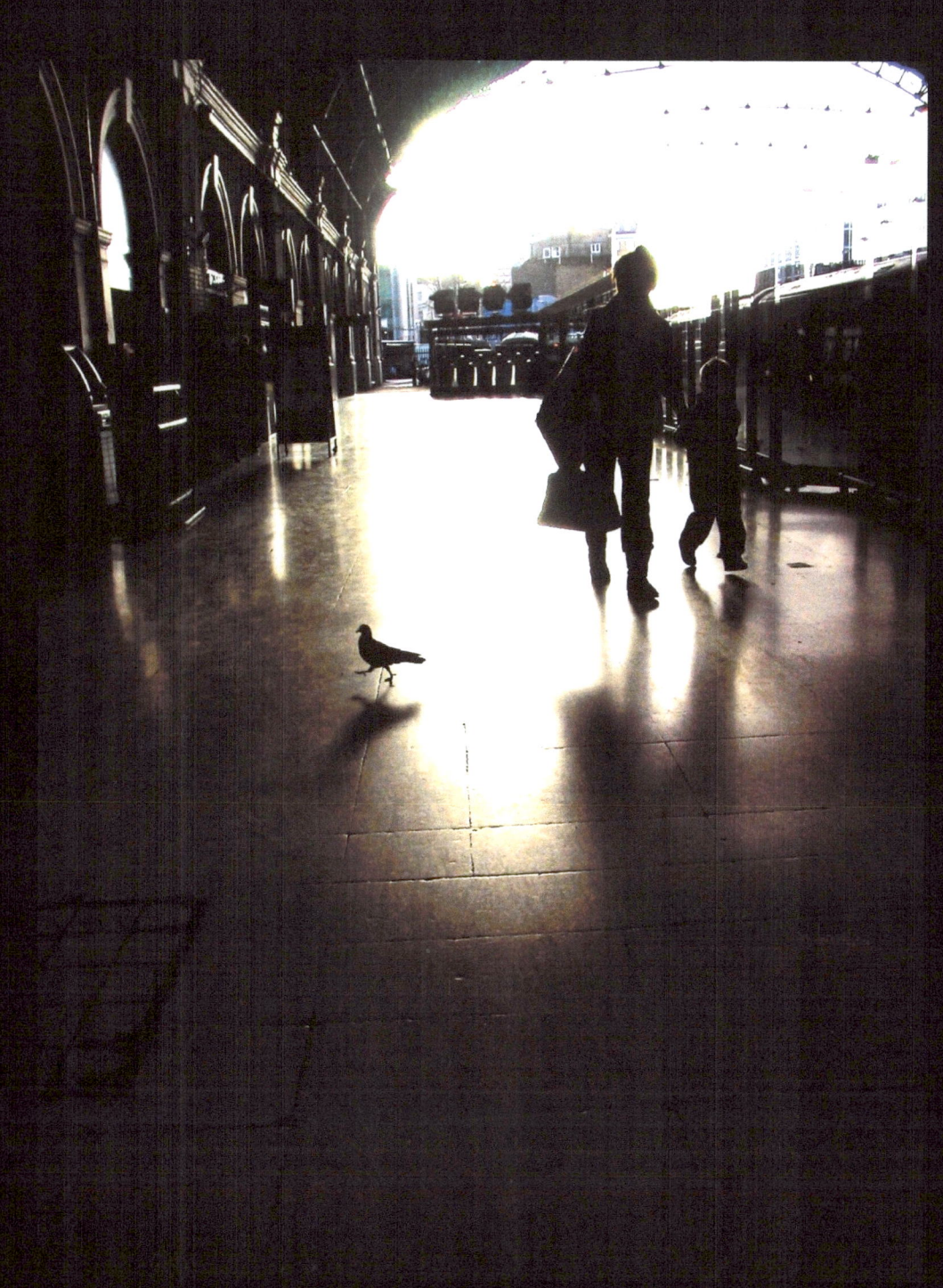

Man's interpretation of religion may form hypothesis of untruths of black & white/ good & bad. Being aware reminds me of what it is like to be a total person & to live as we have God within us.

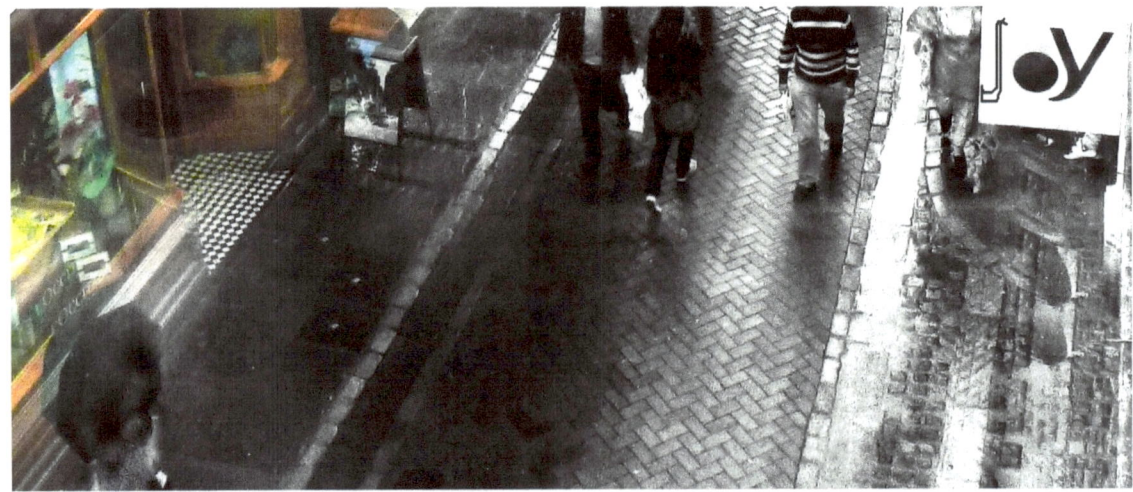

Detail: PILGRIMAGE TO ATONEMENT … traditional Omnipotence . religious icon . urban discourse of discontent.

Power for Self is short lived & self destructive; self absorbed people are blind to their reasons for wanting (needing) power & fool themselves by not acknowledging their insecurities & not looking at "the big picture" of life… yet the byproduct of anger & discord they cause in us pushes us as artists to create some cool art images as avenues of toleration or expressions of rebellion! LOL! xoxox

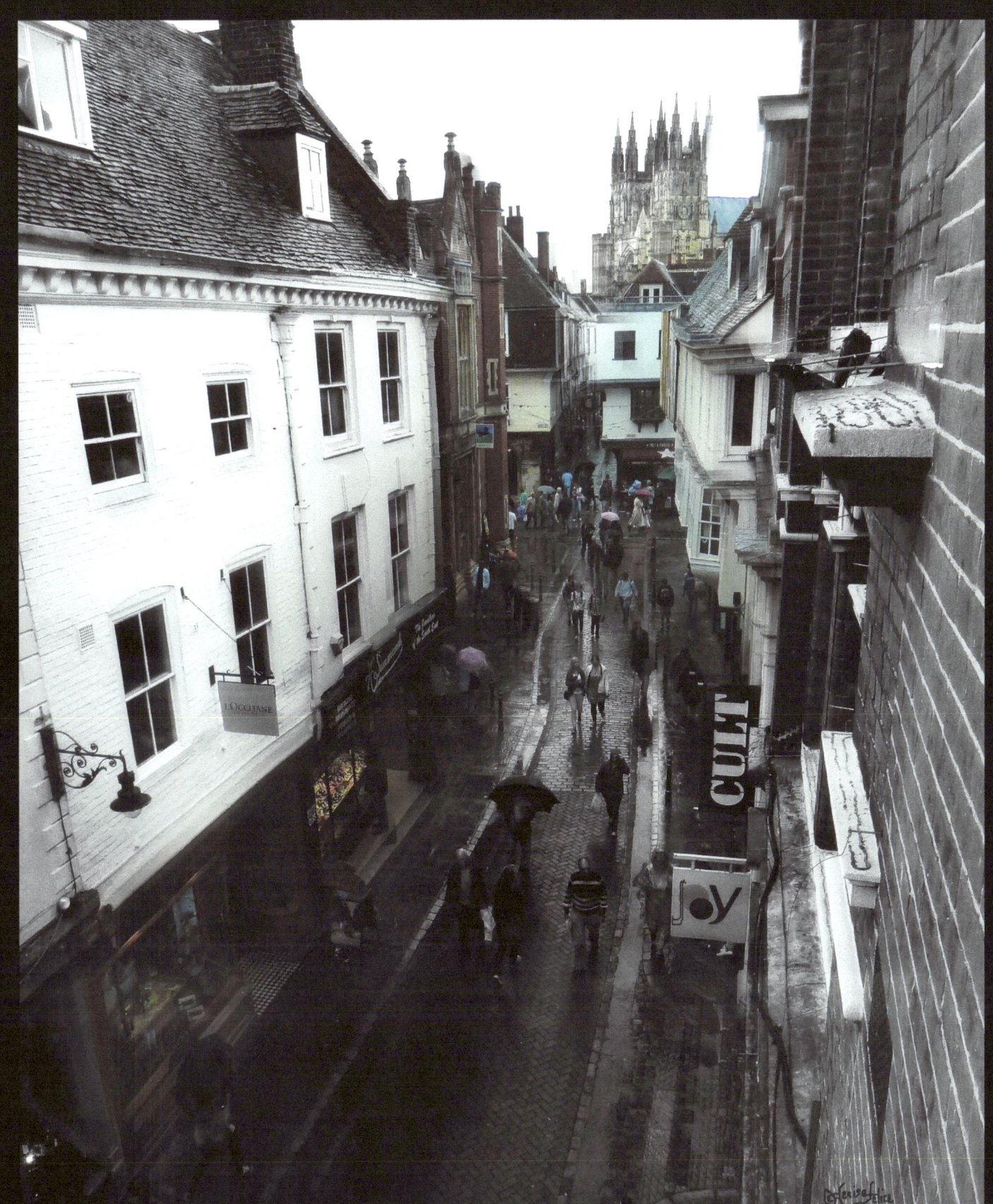

If happiness comes naturally and is uncontrived; then is it not just an illusional state of perception when experienced? ….. or the reverse?

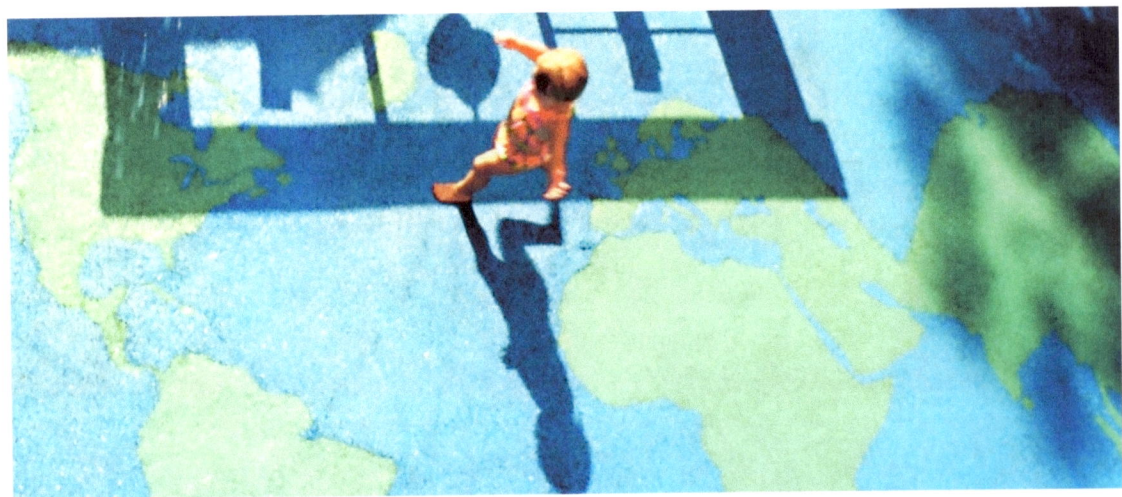

Detail: THE BALANCE OF WORLD PEACE

Thanks my dear friend, it is one of my favorites also; it's about the need for peace:\ I see it as the delicate balance of world affairs, innocence of the new generation which will be effected directly by political strife & also my sadness of intrinsically knowing some children of present time will actually grow up to be adults that disrupt this balance. Optimism should never be shadowed by defeat, so we much strengthen goodness in the young while they are still receptive to empathy.

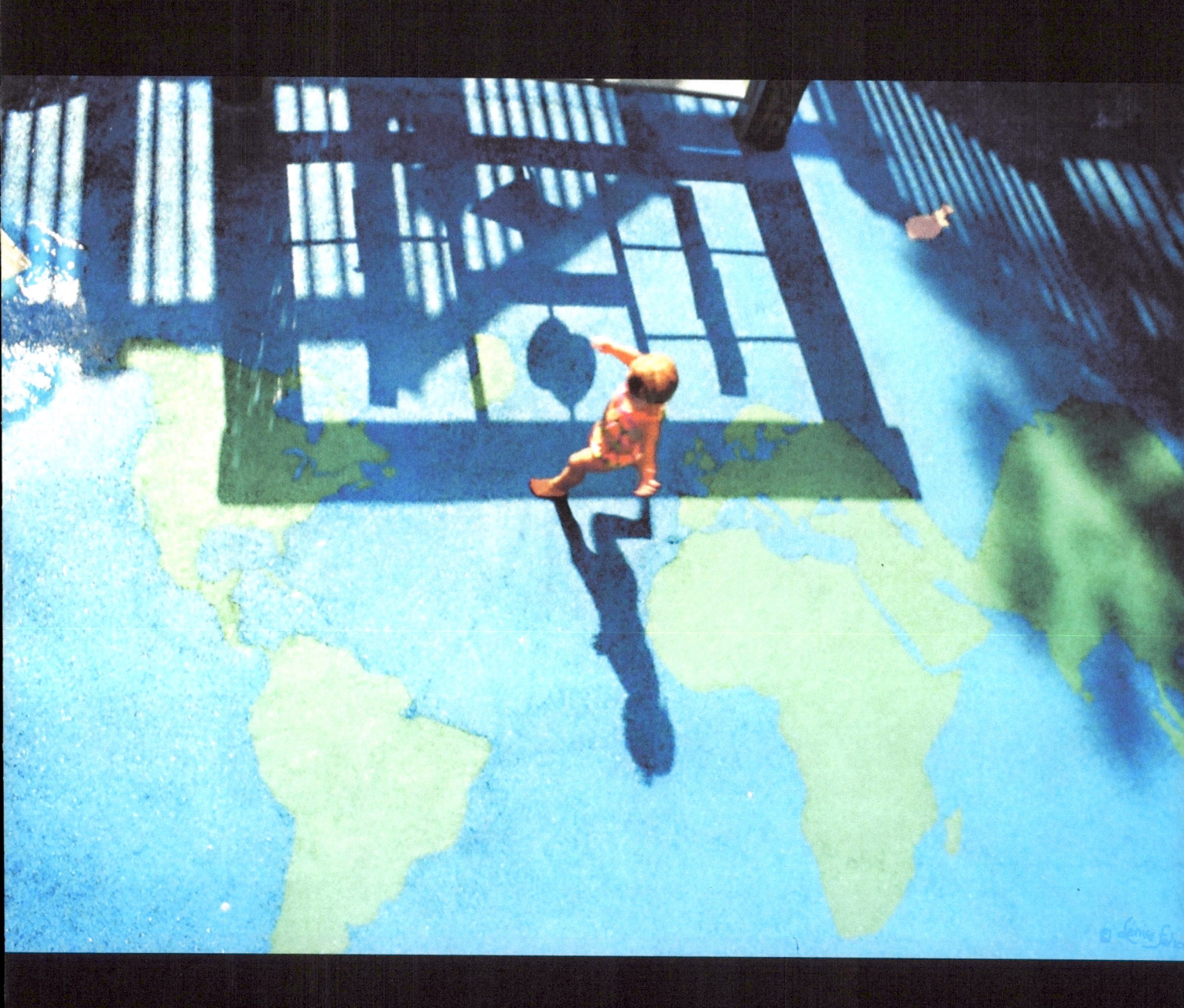

In Modern Society we can walk away from the hurt and not feel guilty; family members do not depend upon each other for life's sustaining tasks. Treasure the ones that treasure us, the ones that hurt us> walk away without needing to battle: they will be ok without us.

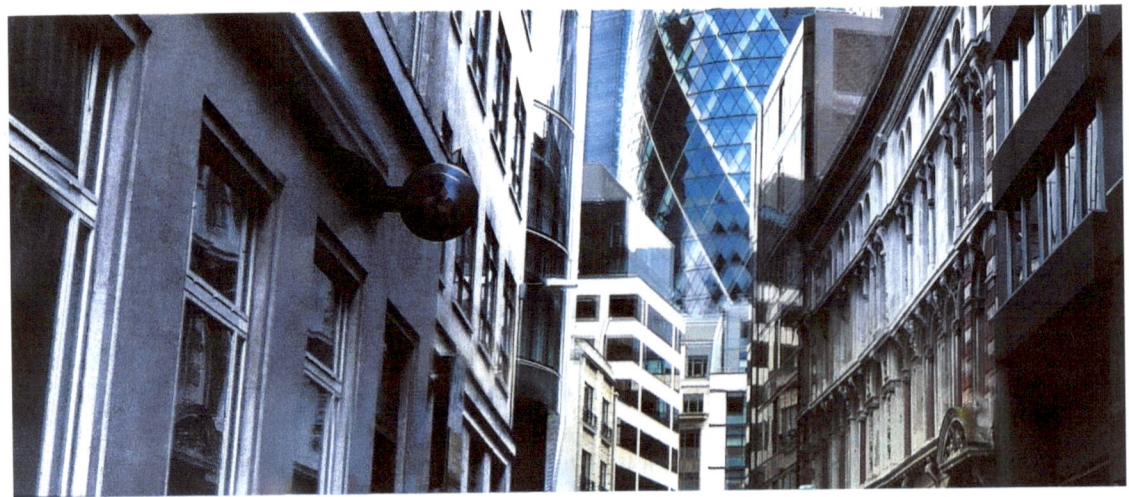

Detail: SHIFTED SELF IDENTITY… contemporary Omniscient . technological lord . urban discourse of discontent.

We can face reality that some people are meaner than others, some prey on the weaker to vent their own aggression, while others may be jealous, and some just enjoy the competitive drama to make life more interesting for themselves and to have something to do (even though they would not admit it).

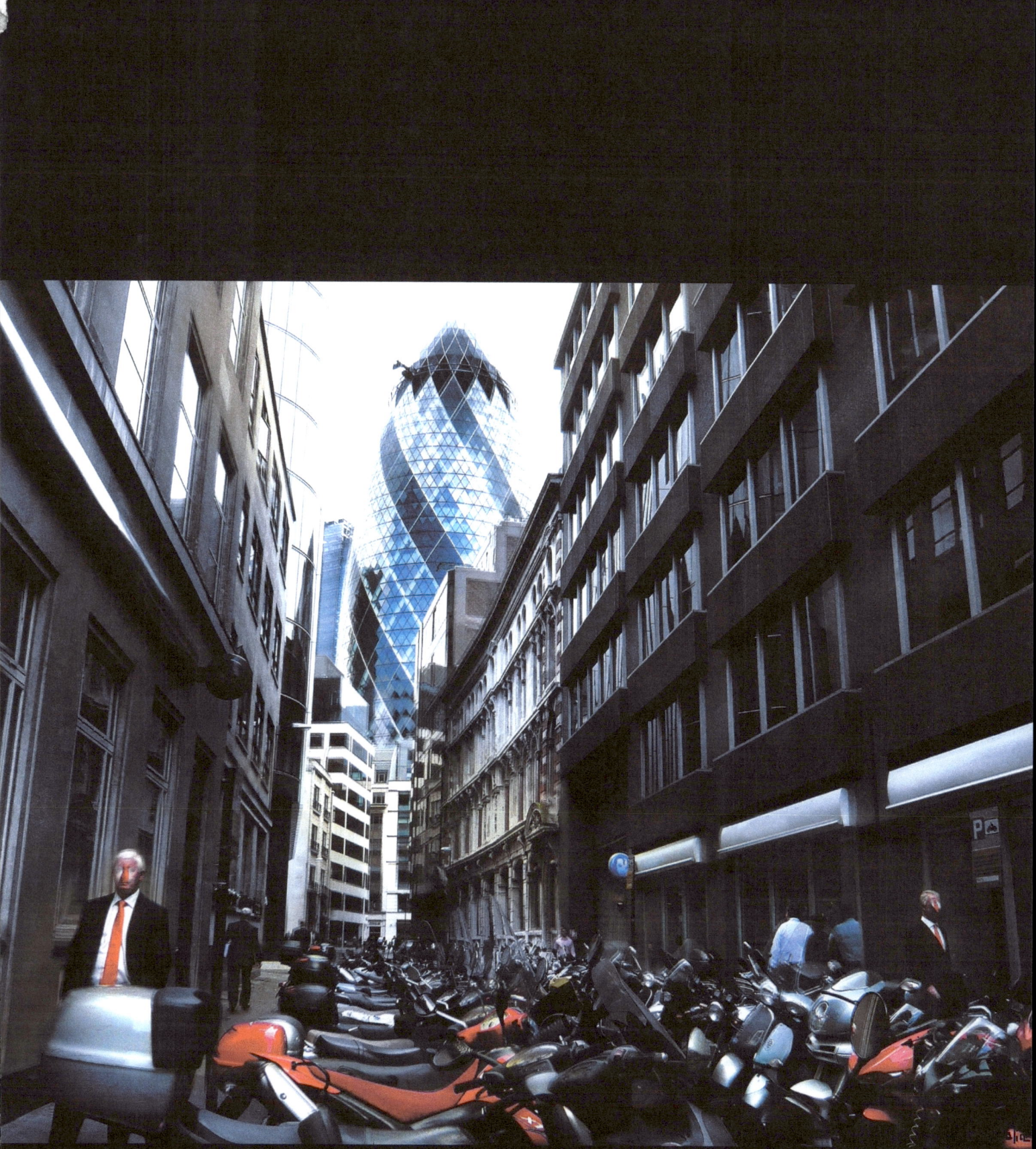

Yes, it's hard to see the big picture of life when small barriers suffocate each breath & prove happiness may be a mere concept. Yet life has to be more than this pain, I am certain.

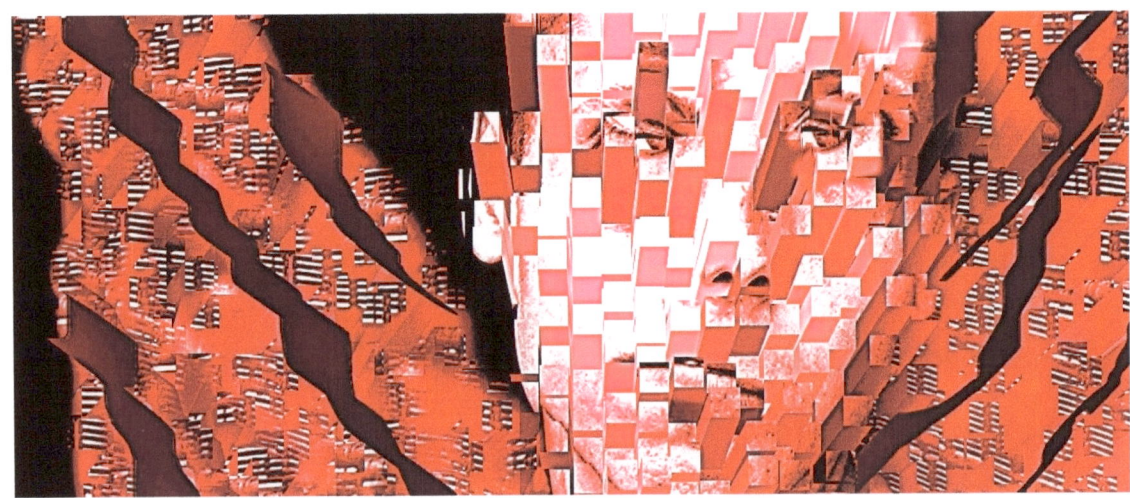

Detail: CITY LIGHTS

I have let go of the 'fear' of uncertainty, misjudgment or my need to make sense of things> I am learning spiritualism may take care of the weak soul if one lets it :) lol! so as not to end on a sappy note> many thanks again for the connection & good thoughts from your garden! Any New Year's resolutions or planned activities? Your extra projects sound fun & rewarding! Almost time to hear fireworks lol! Happiest wishes to you always.

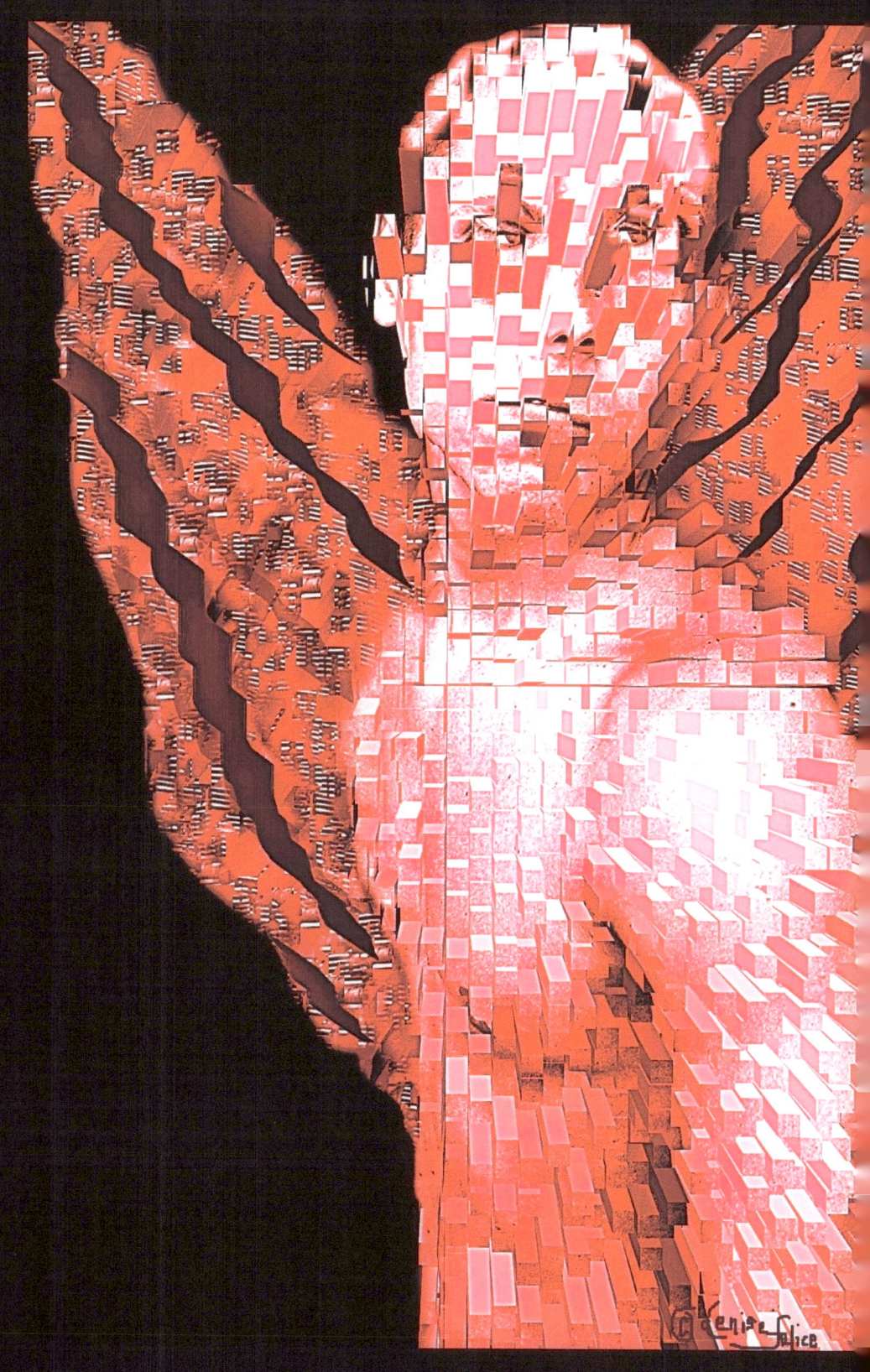

Envision 'the BIG picture of life'; living for not just monetary values & momentary glimpses of success in competition. A broadened vision & outstretched hand will satisfy a deep need for belonging & sense of community.

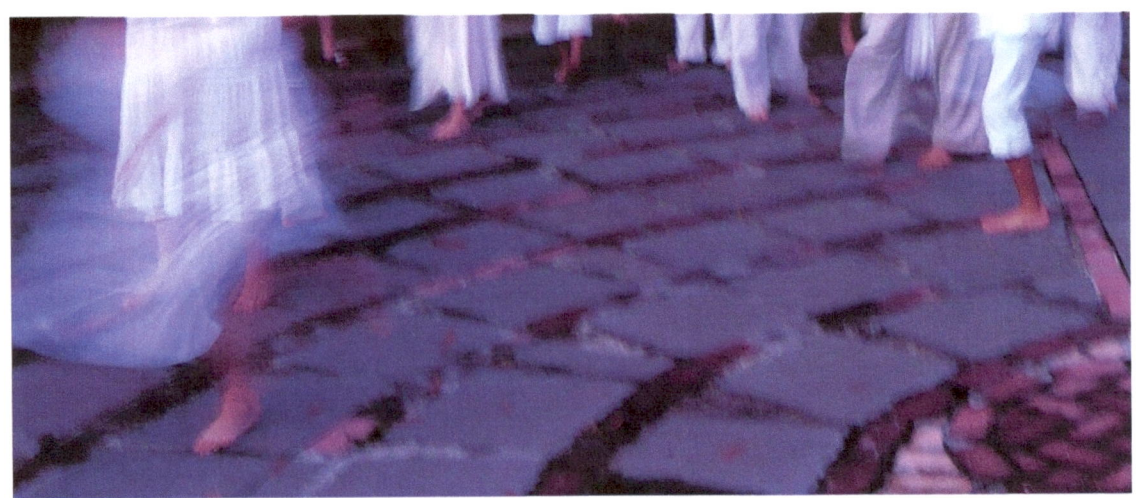

Detail: LABYRINTH GROUND

We do belong in & we are of Humanity. Love with openness, laughter and respect; unfortunately & frustratingly it may not appear as reciprocal, but a seed of caring planted in another will benefit someone in the long run.

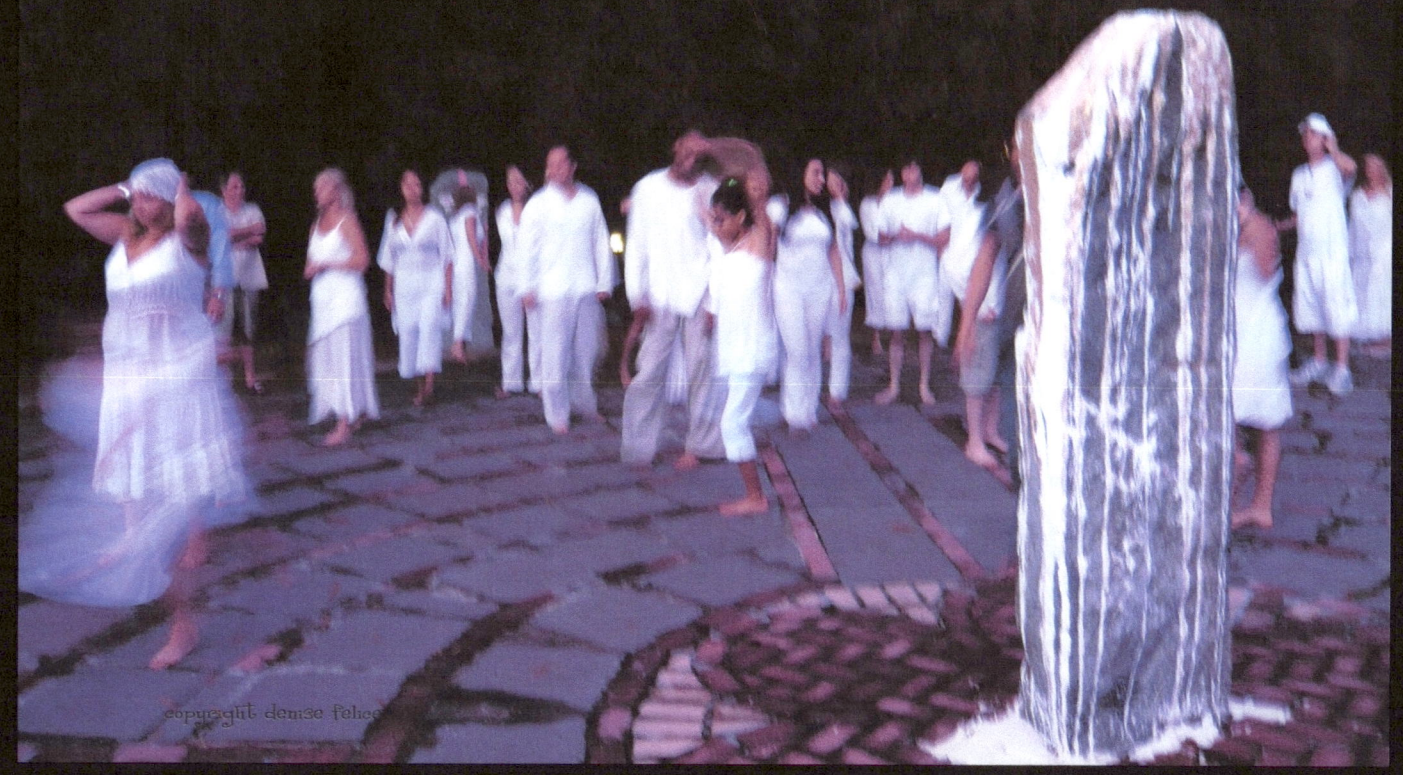

copyright denise felice

we love each other : let not love be a mystery

-denise felice

Let's put up the walls not take the chance of involvement and enjoyment in life's enduring dance. We can stay safely behind in our worlds of woe, pray to fate & destiny to share with us another future blow.

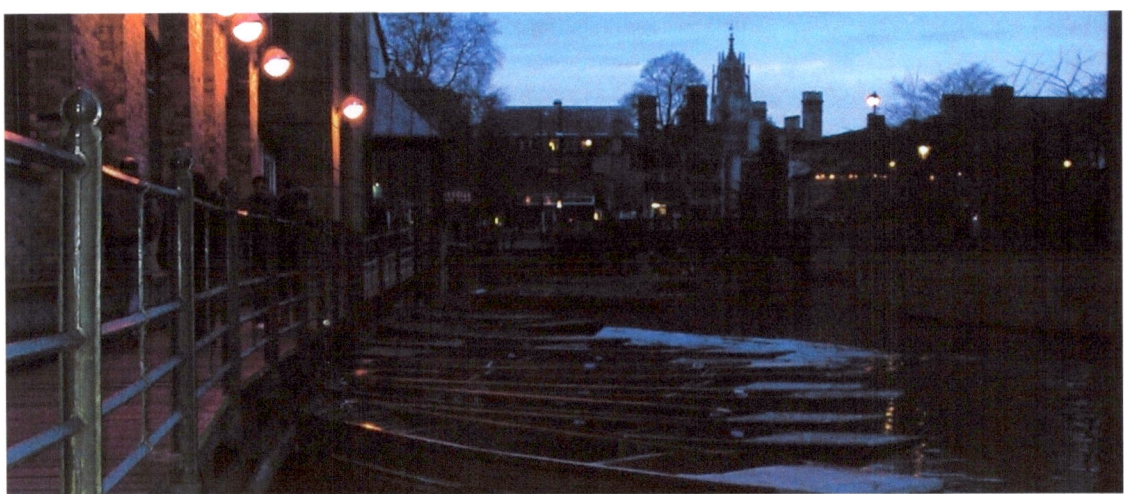

Detail: LOST SONNETS

'Anything is possible' you say, yet you talk in riddles...since we've reunited I haven't smiled...I don't know if it is your sadness or me knowing our distance will only grow further. You say there's hope & we must strive for freedom to allow love to move us back to each other... How?> Please explain?

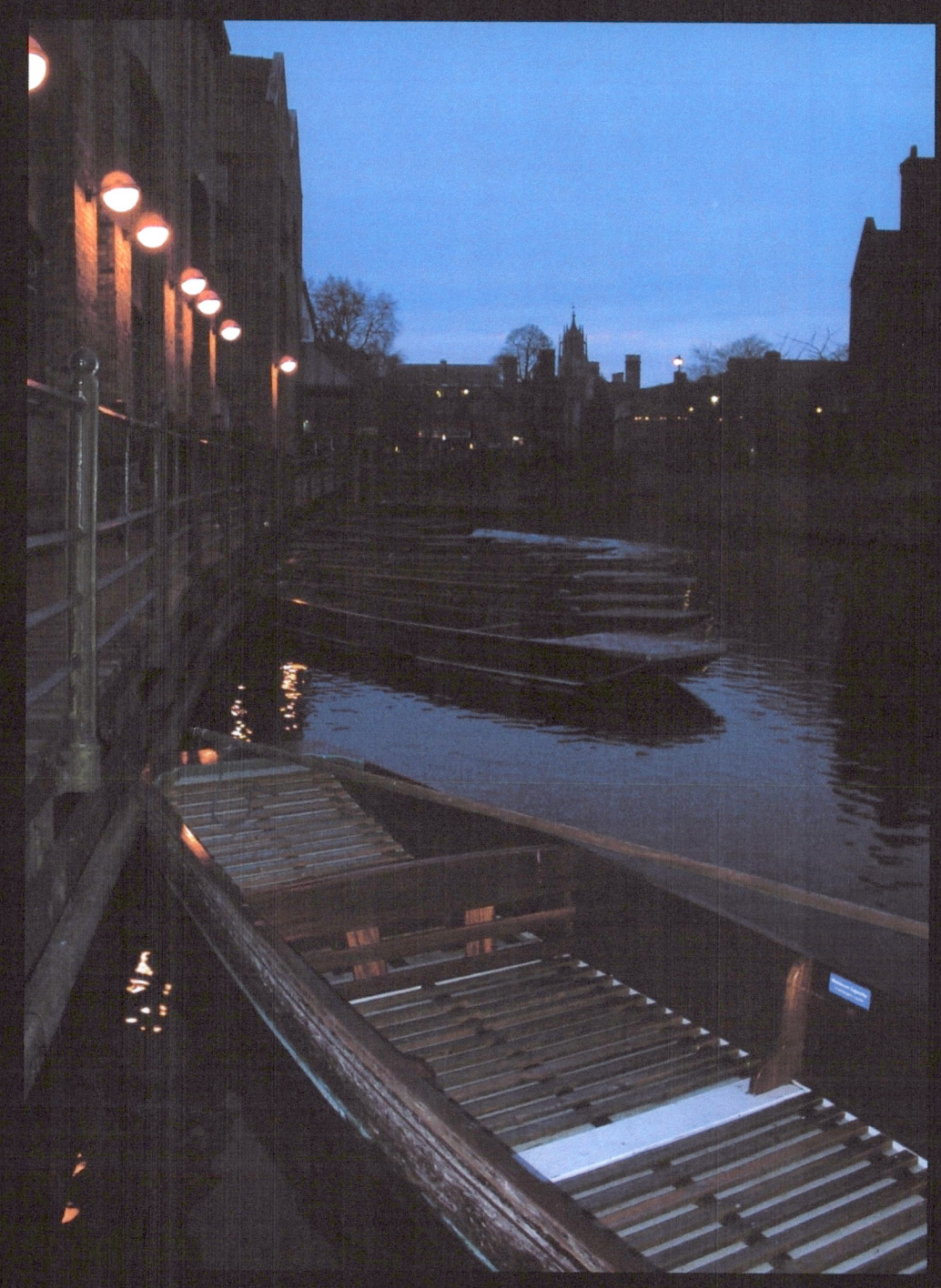

For some have a life's commitment filled with devotion, nurturing & passion afire; considered not a waste of a lifetime, frivolous or supercilious desire.

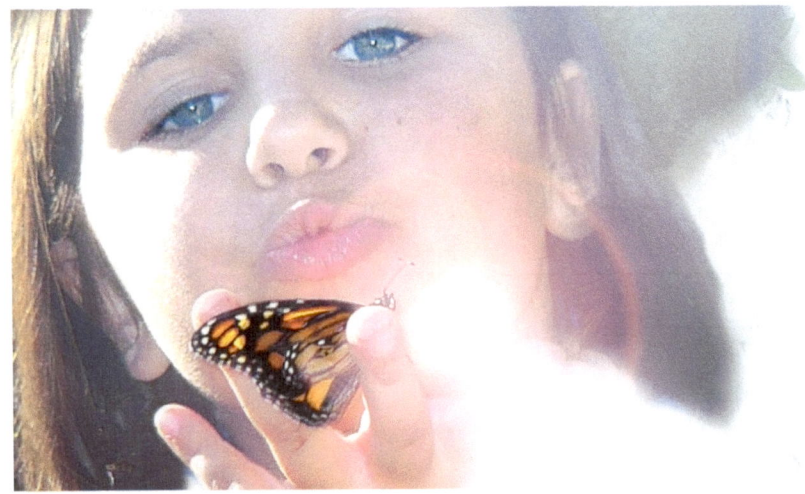

Detail: INTRINSIC APPRECIATION

I am fortunate to have walked with my grandparents across their acres of fruit trees and endless gardens of blossoms. Their shared laughter & unspoken warmth during countless days together nurturing their garden,.. symbolizing their life of nurturing each other & the beauty of love.

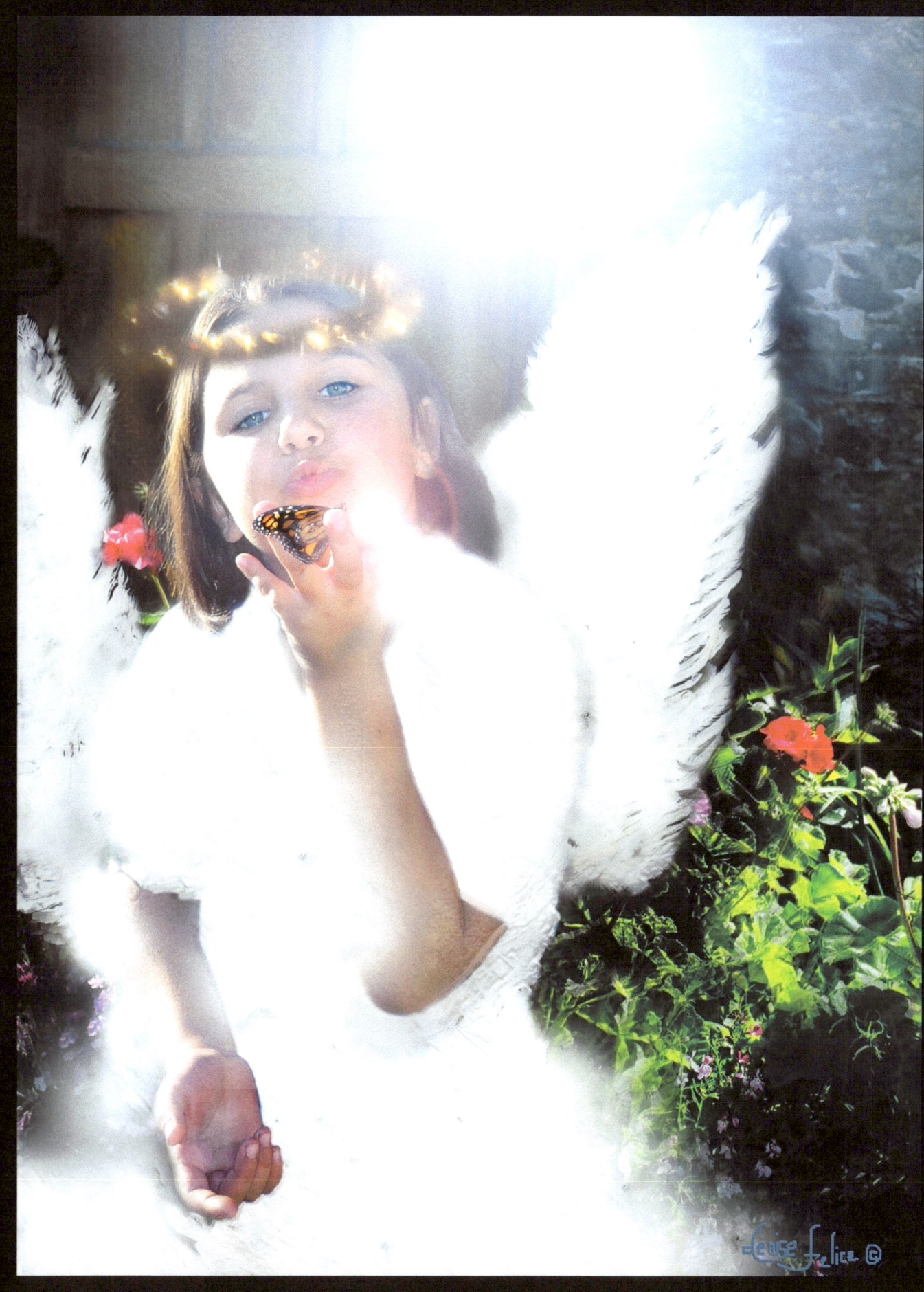

We question reality, asking is it chance or fate? never appreciating ourselves or our ability to love…vanishing moments, lost connections, losing inner passion… insecurity wins at an astounding rate.

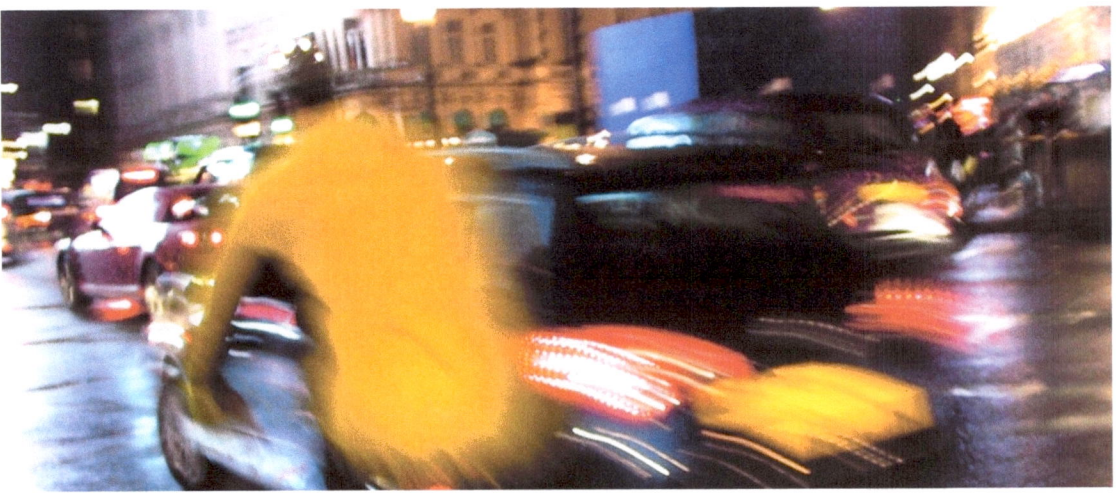

Detail: RACING TIME

life is so strange… i loathe when the past just seems like a memory that never actually occurred. I hope your life is back to a tangible/ tactile form of happiness… the imaginary can only take us into sanity just so far! I am so glad you are connected back to home, bittersweet yet directed towards fulfillment :)

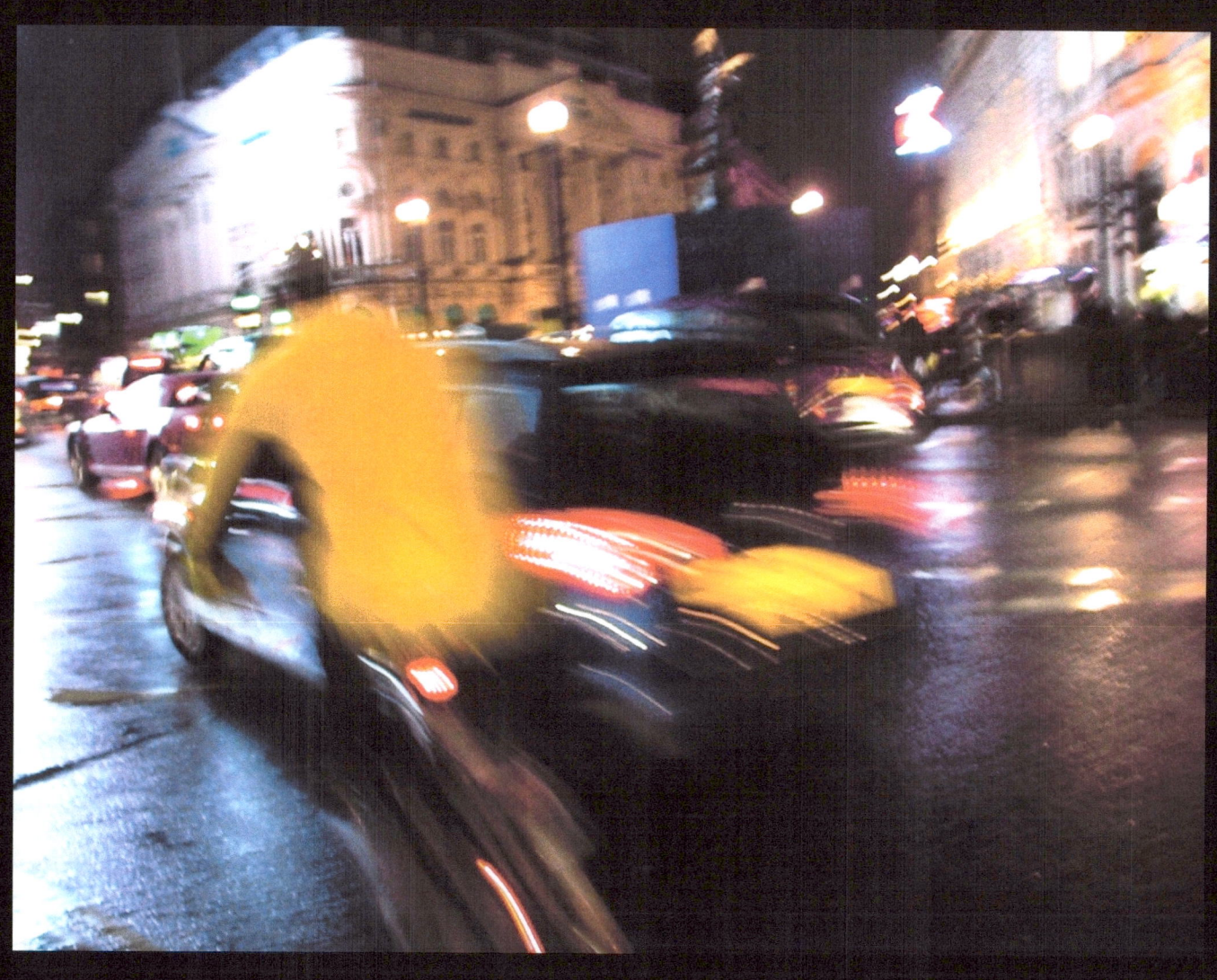

Dissatisfaction of true love, destroyed by doubt and fear of rejection, reeks havoc in our souls yet we accept as destiny; making excuses while sacrificing true happiness in search for materialistic perfection.

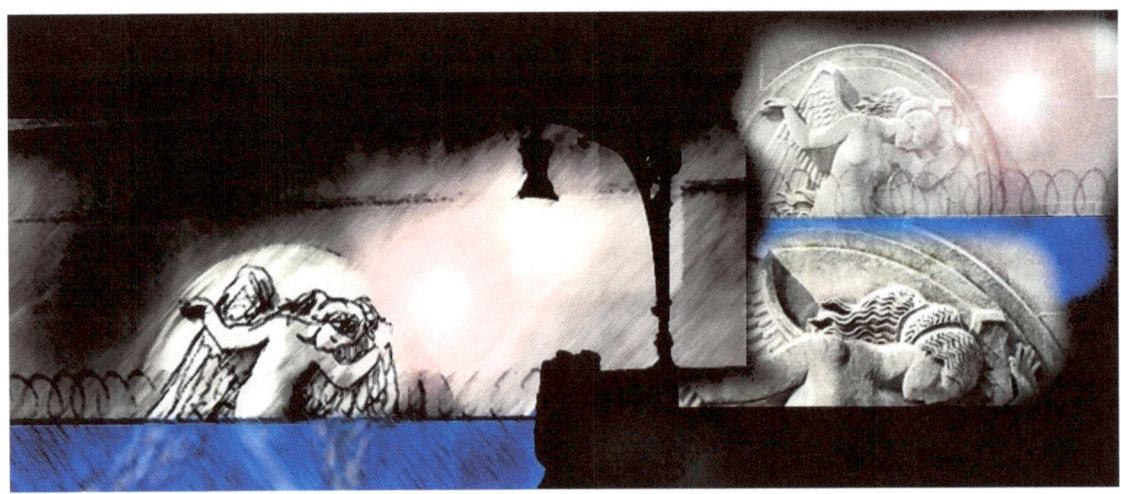

Detail: NYC BARBEDWIRE FREE

I'm hoping you may appreciate me. I believe in you, not the quandaries & doubts which must be dissected … life is short, sharing happiness instead of second guessing if it is deserving, must take precedent over our insecurities and find it's place in our busy lives.

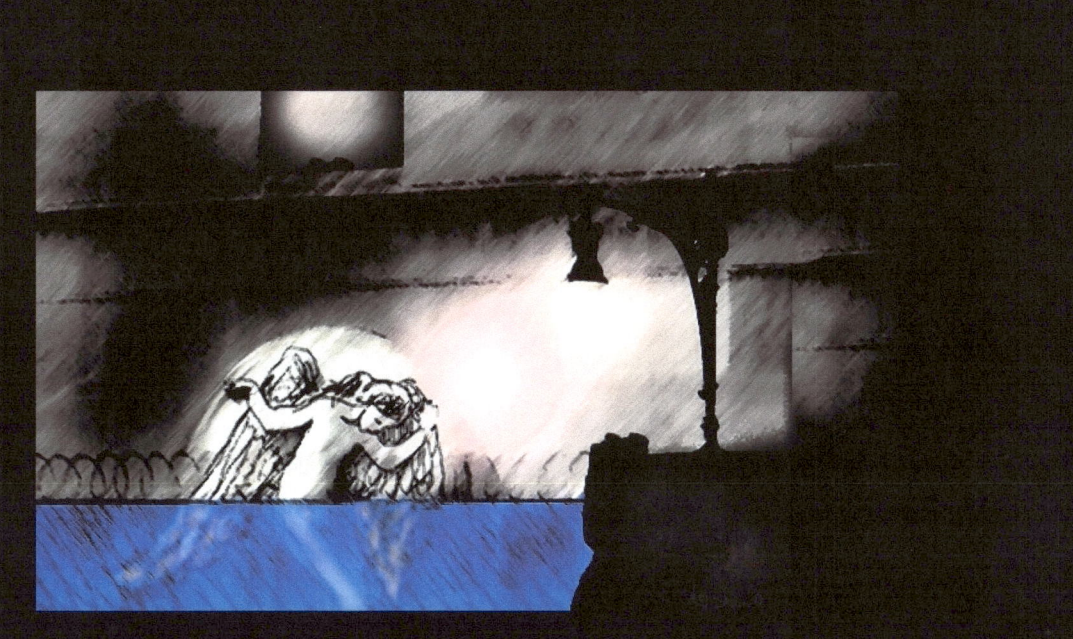

Painful breakdown of communication with misinterpretation of motives appear as lies, lovers can choose to rectify with heard voice, or accept with defeat & demise.

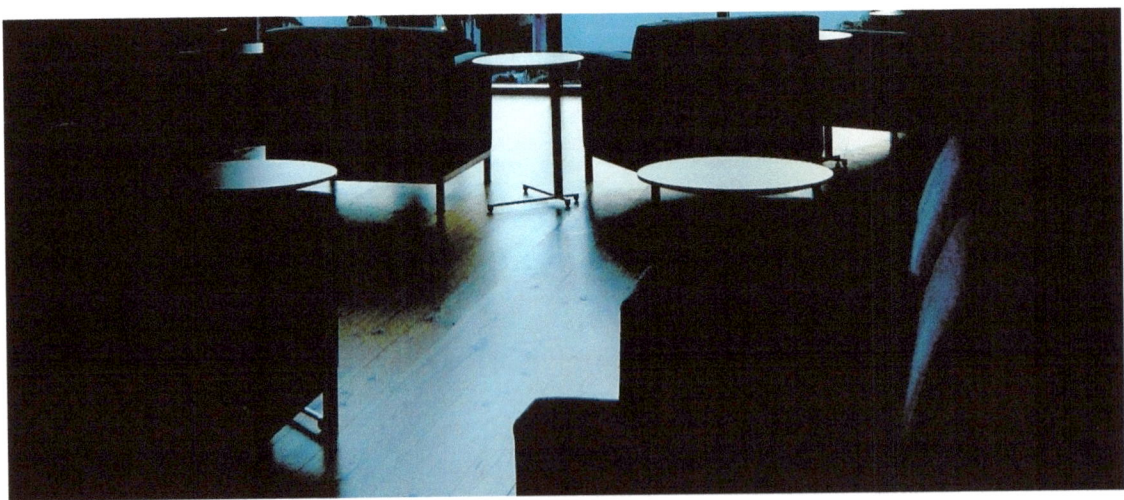

Detail: DIMENSIONS OF SOCIAL DISTANCE

A LESSON:
...learn?... learn not to fight back or to feed you fuel?> ... to just walk away to regain my pride, wipe my tears and preserve my emotional health/ sometimes there is no way to figure the situation out, we just make excuses for how we treat each other... 'hoping the future will heal the relationship'.

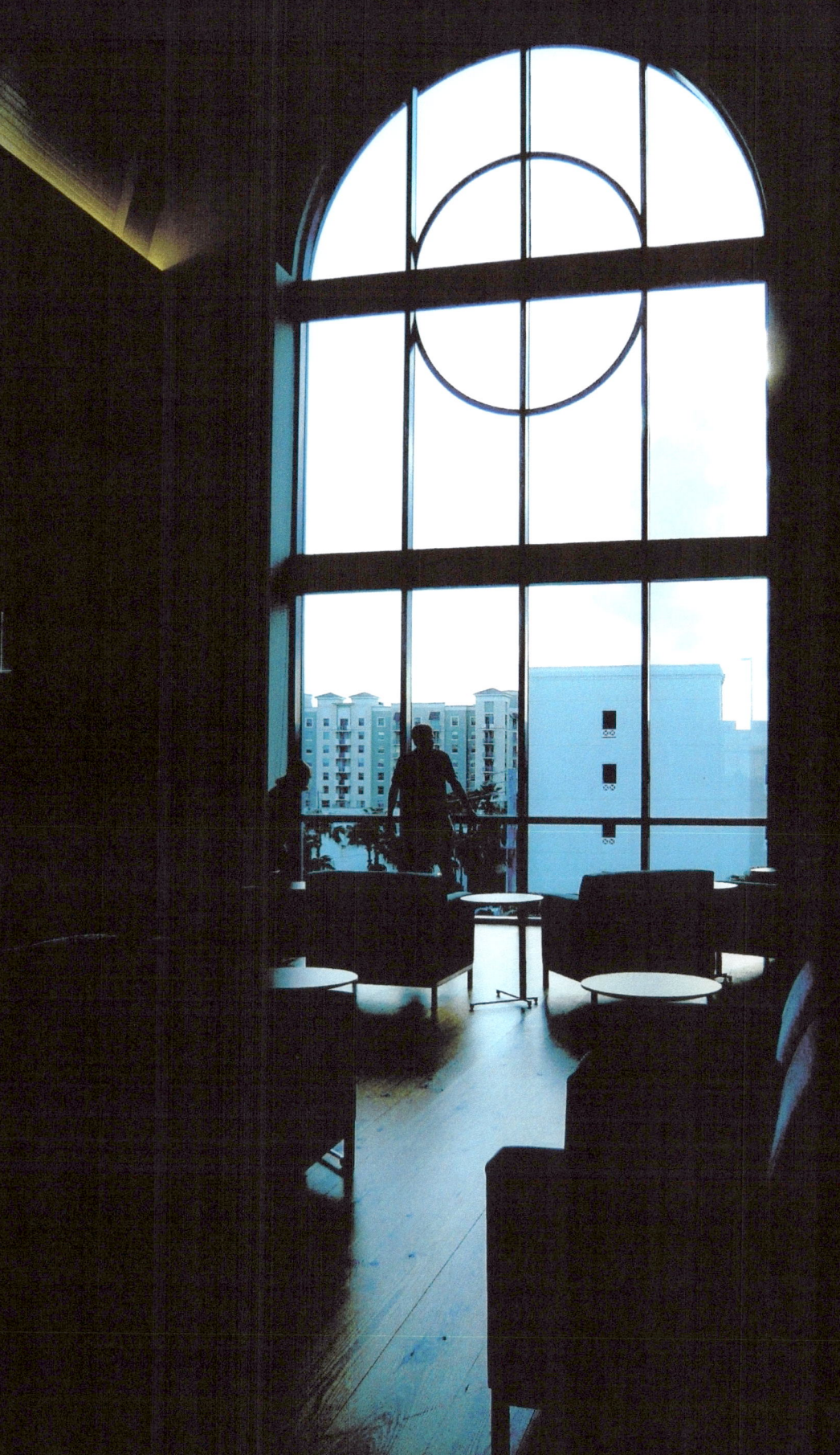

Deep rooted & grown without conscious endeavor, hurtful transference surfaces as division, yet together as one we can chose to have love flourish with sentiment & pleasure.

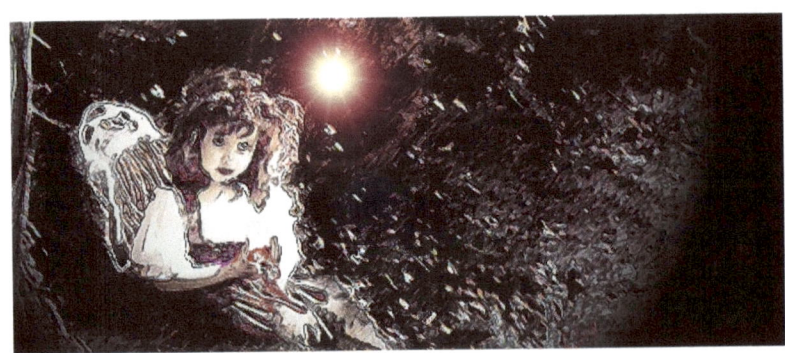

Detail: FOREST ANGEL

"I'll call you", "I'll answer"> probabilities (only) Your save-me glance to me was heartwarming & familiar as if we were friends for years. I wish we would have spoken so we could have laughed about the evening as promised in our deal…the over zealous crowd, I felt as if I was in a cartoon where the characters were tossed around like objects in a windstorm> I am hoping the experience didn't take a toll on you also. I am very sorry… overwhelming, something I had not intended; how you had to put up with the commotion & hundreds of people. I too may have become one of them, swallowed up by the energy of motion, inadvertently…I apologize for not being strong enough to remove ourselves from the unnecessary pull of others during the evening. I wonder if we would have met on common ground things would have gone more smoothly? A chance at fate, or possibly fate took over & our souls stayed sheltered within.

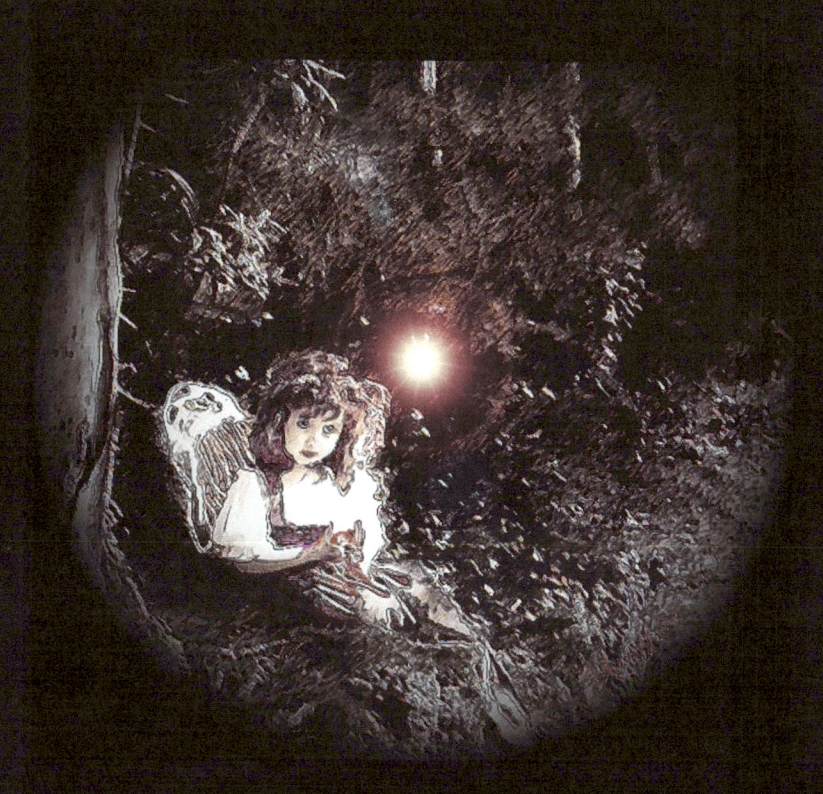

This discovery has begun, true intimacy more than just near, and for you & I to nurture, if we chose, without walls sharing our entire selves while letting go of expectation, judgment and fear.

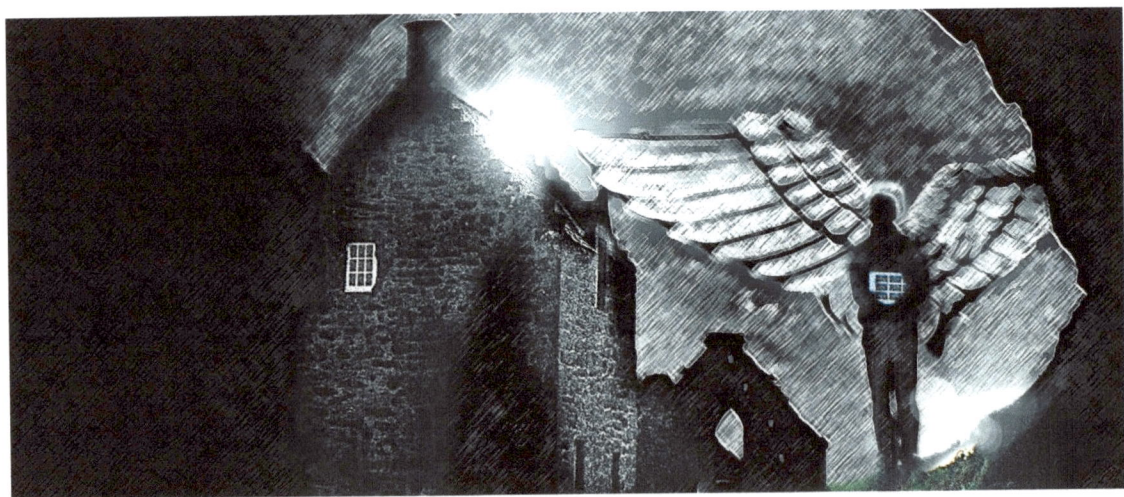

Detail: RUINS REVISITED REVITALIZED

Yes, I feel you always… A great day, I have been writing & writing, would you like to join me ;)…it is so confusing & in circles, yet I know you will understand it! >let's brainstorm for a venture>> this secret>>go full force/+ energy and our ability to adapt to any situation will show direction>>start planning together by opening our minds to the endless possibilities of creativity with the spectrum of emotional & intellectual voice!!!!

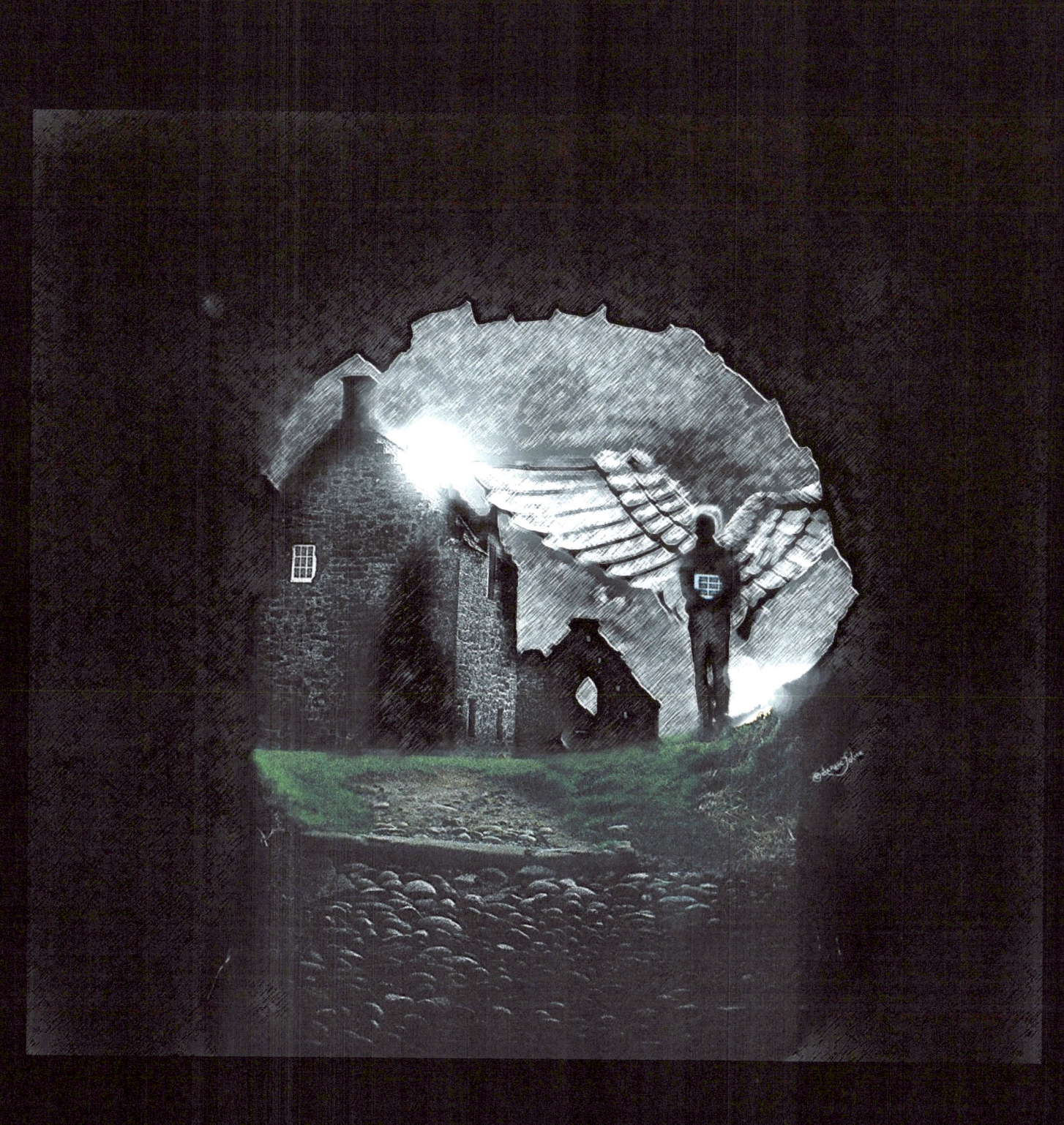

To let hearts take an unbridled path nourishing love's gifts received without hesitation, realizing blindness is actual sight, mutual awareness is intrinsic/ never a creation.

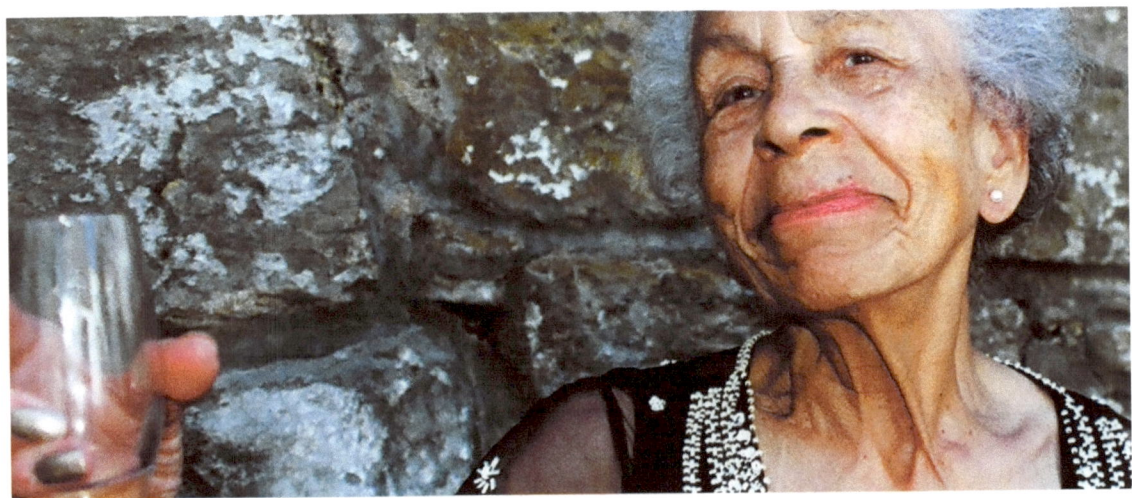

Detail: CHEERS TO LIFE & LOVE!

…such is wonderful, this creative process, possibly like one writes a song or music? Yes, this will have to be a joint venture, since I will not be there in person, I can instruct you only in part… the next step would be for you to let it become alive from within. Understanding & Orchestrating; an international collaboration with two points of view yet one intention… an image of intrinsic emotional fusion!

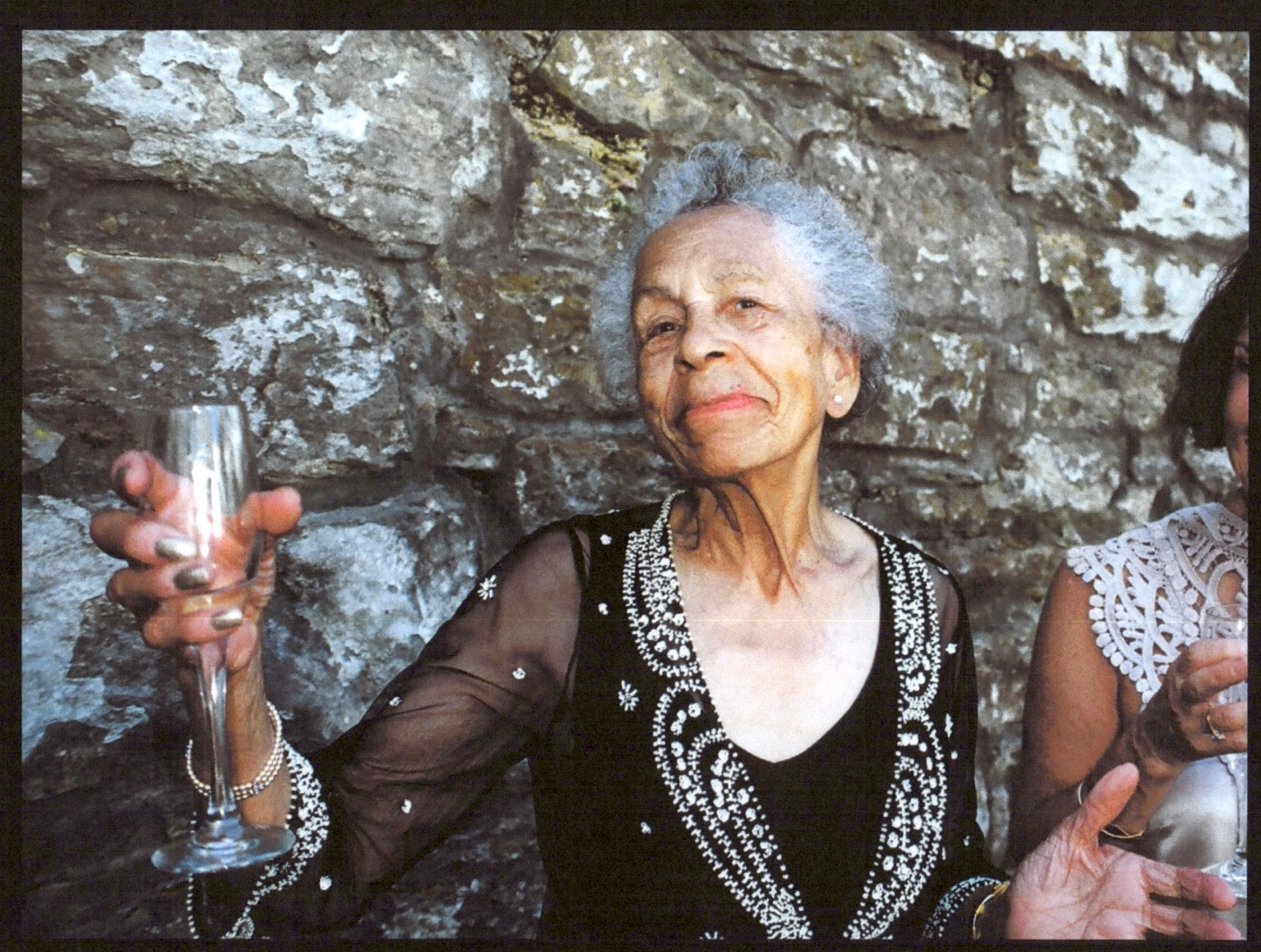

The existence of a life shared in compassion & strength is cast over the edge propelled by judgmental mistrust & longing for youth. Reverence of ideal epitome creates longings not satisfaction, as we repeat the same patterns believing as truth.

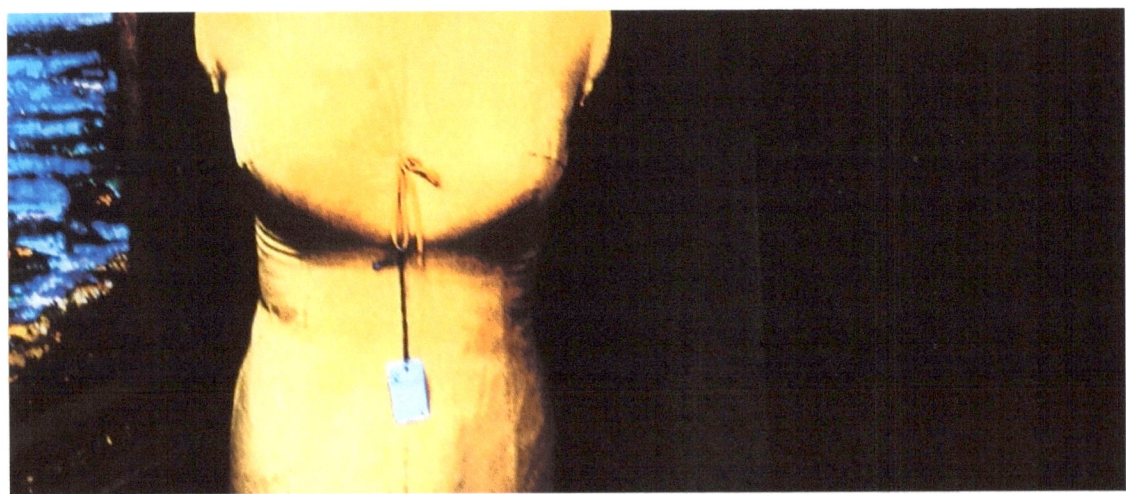

Detail: DISPOSABLE AMERICAN DREAM

To myself I will whisper in my mind… "Not as surrender, oddly I do concur any holiday celebrating love & caring is a wonderful proclamation of goodwill, even to one without a partner."… which will give me the courage to say to you>> Goodbye emotionally, intellectually & physically beautiful man. Your texts, phone calls, and timing are too confusing. It is Valentine's Day & I am alone.
Today I will be a realist. I cannot be part of a one-sided relationship with the hope of the other person one day caring about me. You have my email if you would ever want to write & talk about life. Best wishes to you for all good things to come to you in life.

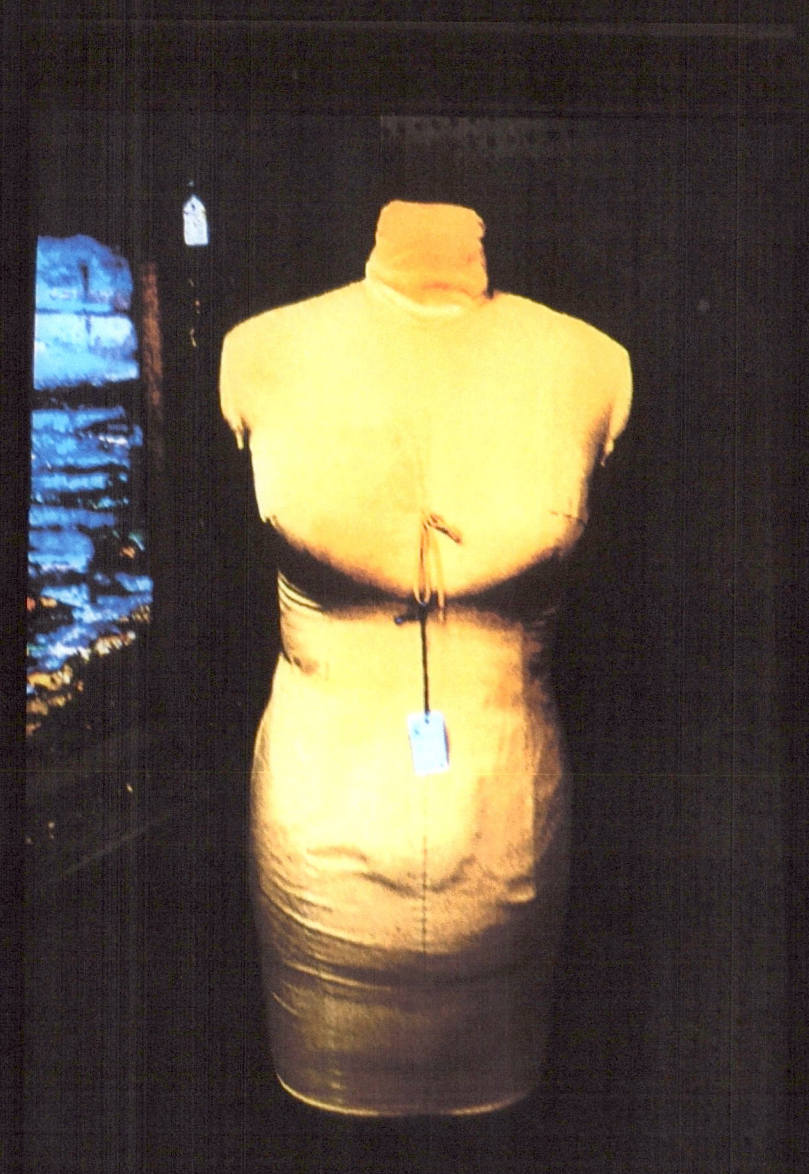

Yet a lifetime of learning from our past to retreat, to wonder what's next & what we must chance, furthers stark isolation never romance. It is a game of wager, not love, again & again to role play in anticipation of ultimate defeat.

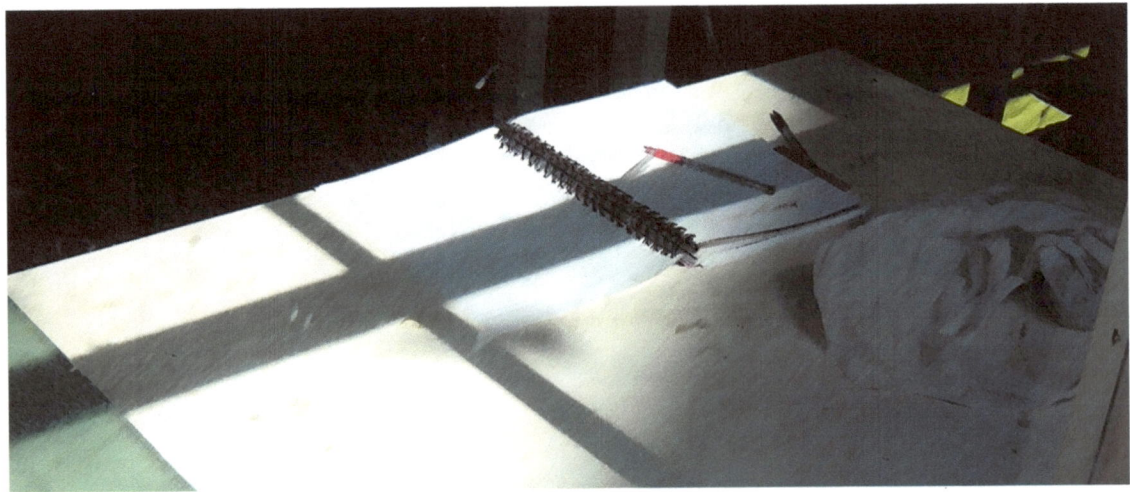

Detail: PLEASE TELL ME YOUR SECRETS

Faults are fine and part of the human experience, yet in an equal relationship both partners should have concern for one another. I prefer discussions NOT common debates> discussions are wonderful & create understanding to reach a more intimate level of the way a person feels.

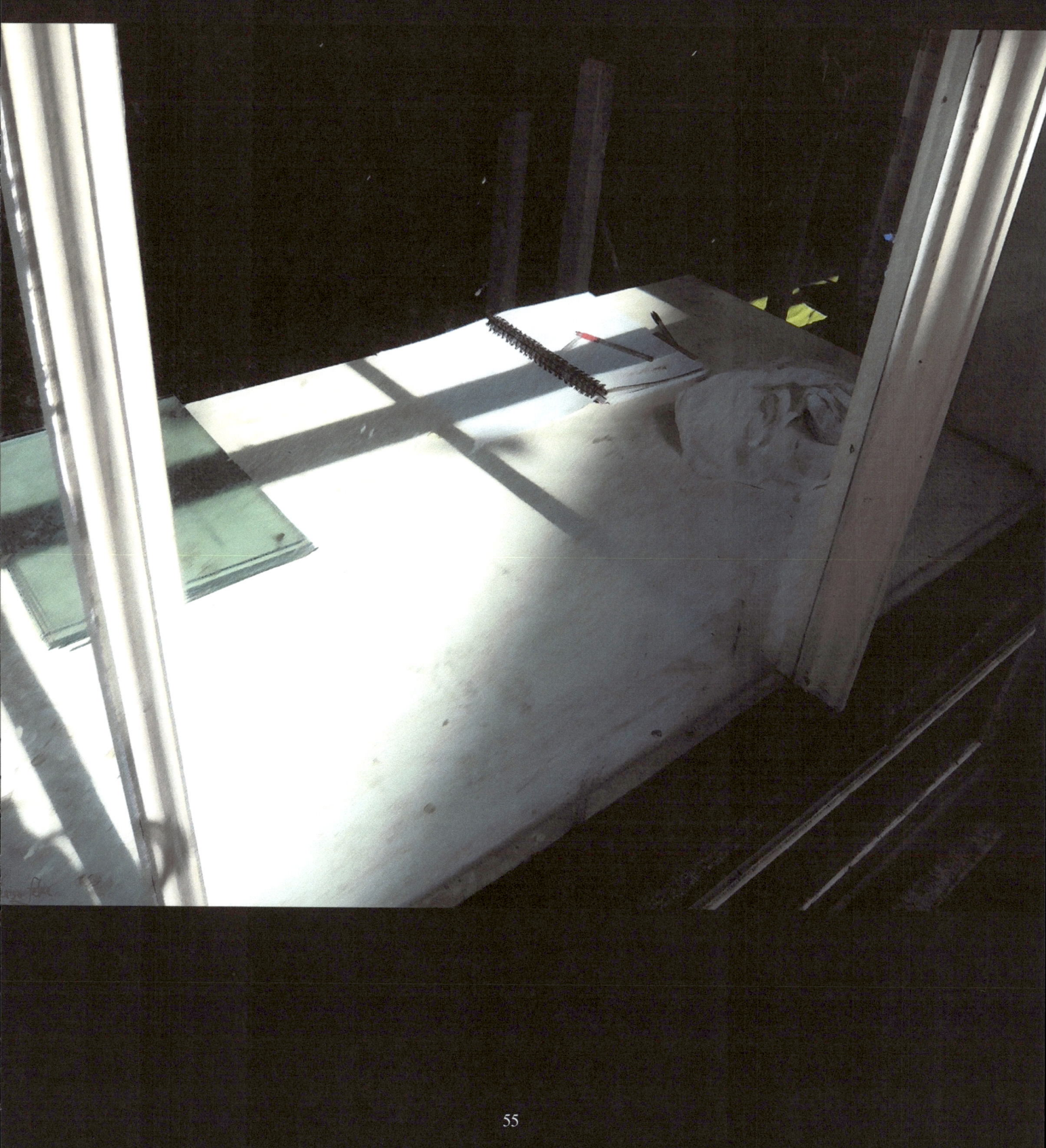

From within are cries for this solitude to not consume, for when fear pushes we surrender to self hate. Cerebral intelligence then follows as we lock our hearts in self protection with false self love to reciprocate.

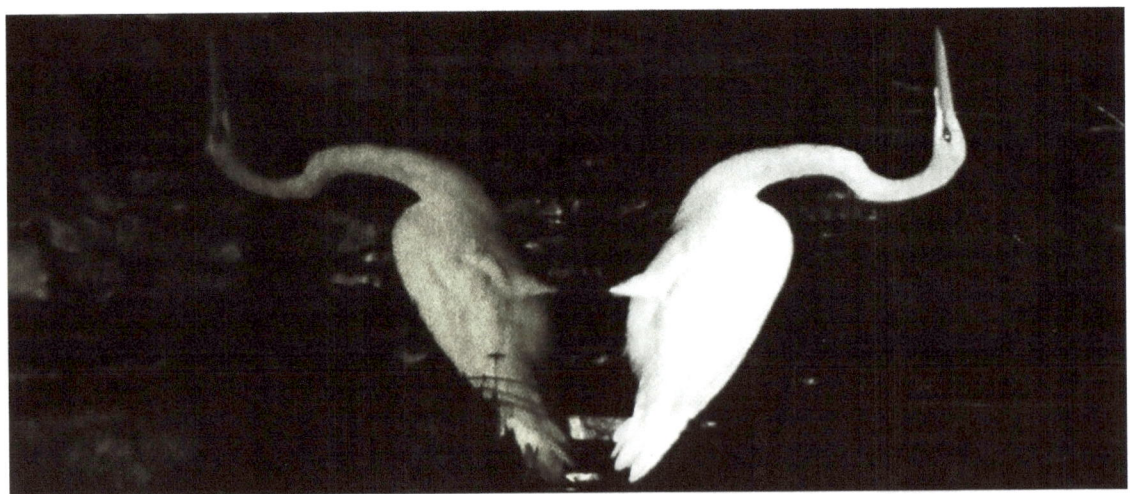

Detail: MYSTIC EGRET… Dichotomy of the spirit and actual form; existence/ introspective stillness yet the waters are murky and can include danger if one stays too long without defenses.

Friday night was the start of a turning point in my life, not an awakening for I was always aware of the turmoil I was in, but rather external environmental changes are pushing me away from demons> actually extinguishing my tolerance level for the demons I had inside myself; ones which I was before too weak to fight.

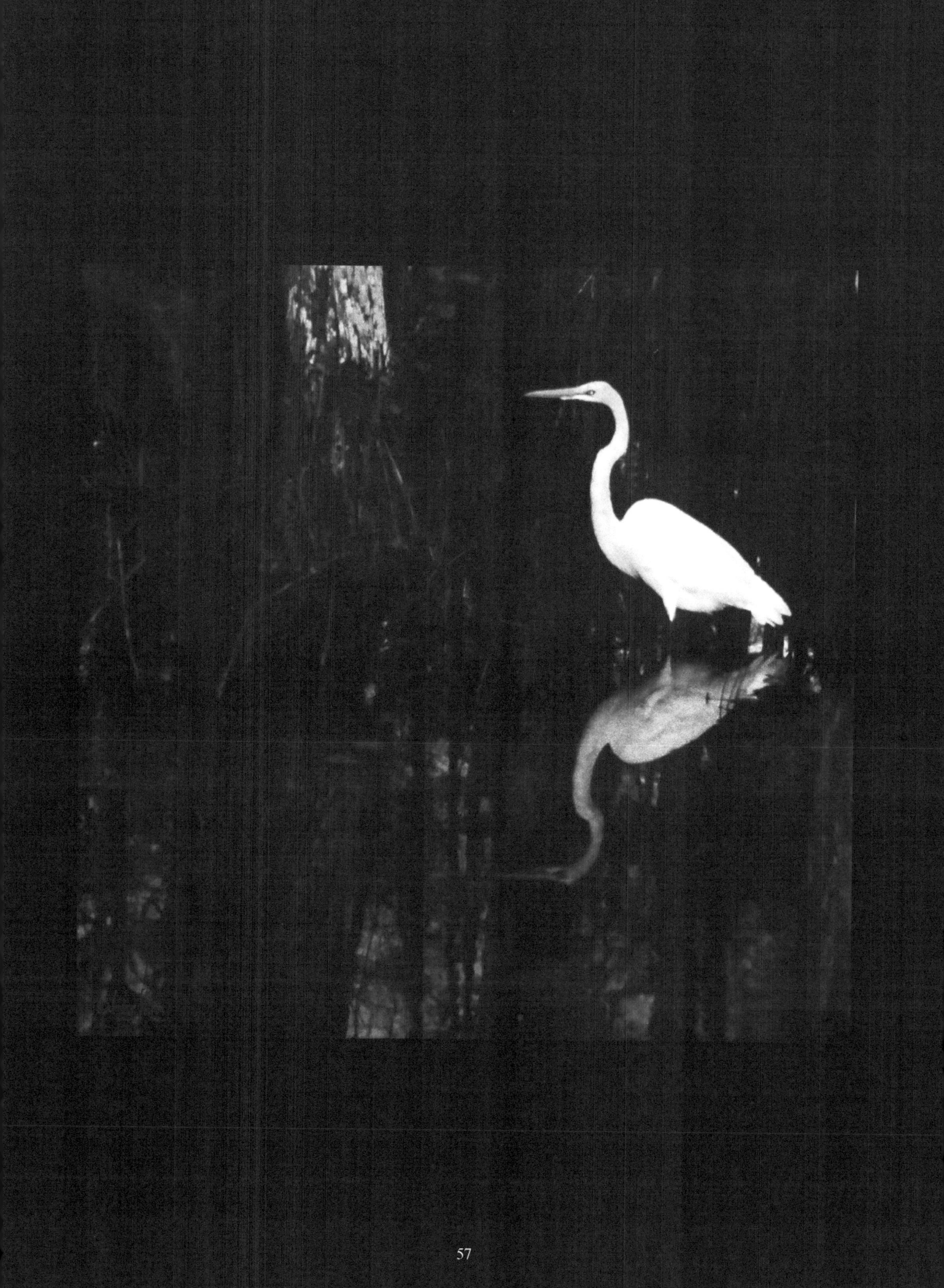

All the while, as fate always knew with deep understanding why, we repeat which we have pre-wrote to create a future of misgiving, with paralysis we see yet cannot care for our spirit or appreciate the life we are living.

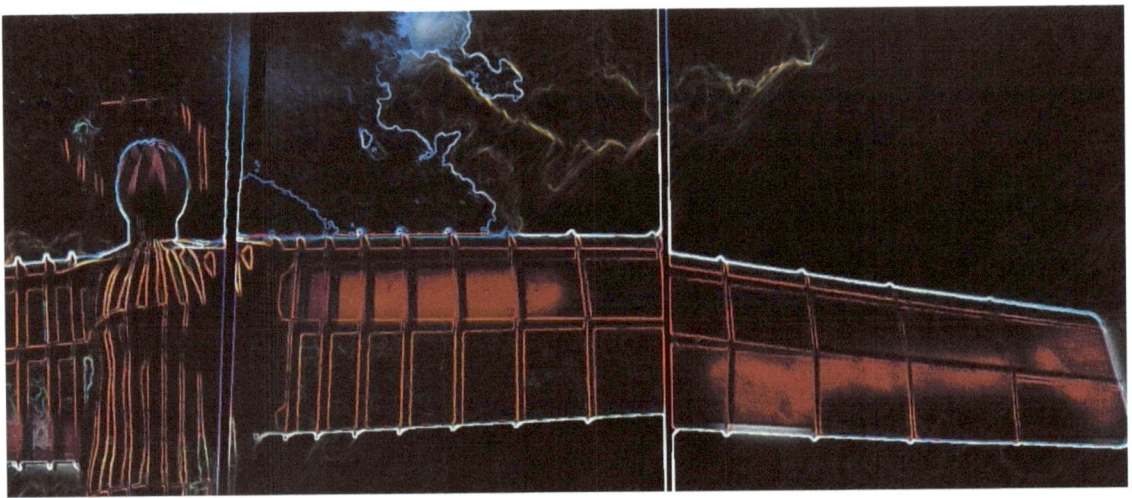

Detail: STEADFAST

I've learn to detach and now instead of trying to understand or explain to others... appreciation, honest acceptance/ no retaliation or thought of revenge, remorseful possibly until fully healed...; I am just letting it go and breathing in life again... life value is now felt / balance and knowledge that life is a gift.

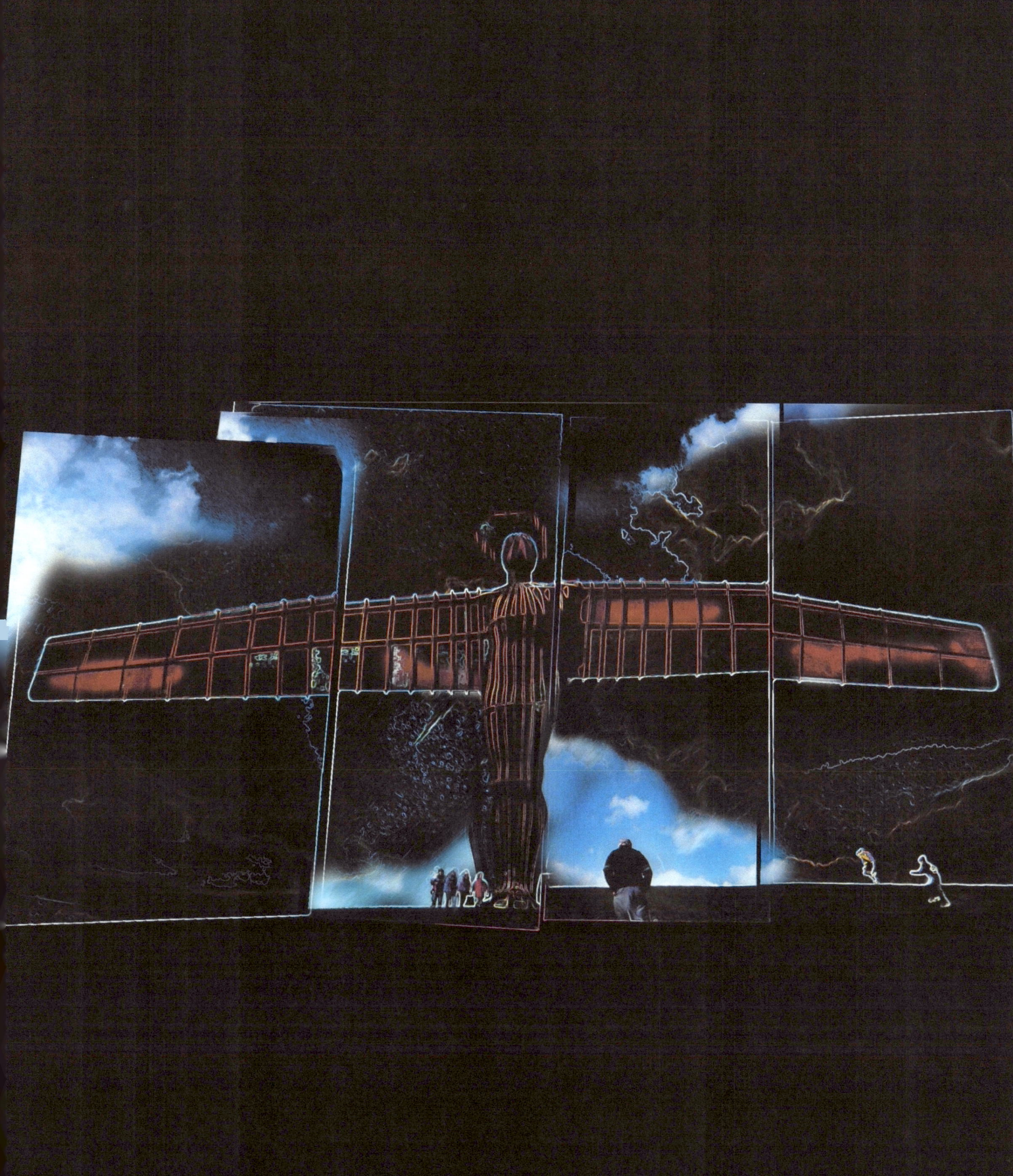

When one loves to love, without greed, miracles are not far behind... Life as its' self becomes a miracle when we open our eyes forgetting ourselves, our pasts, and our minds...

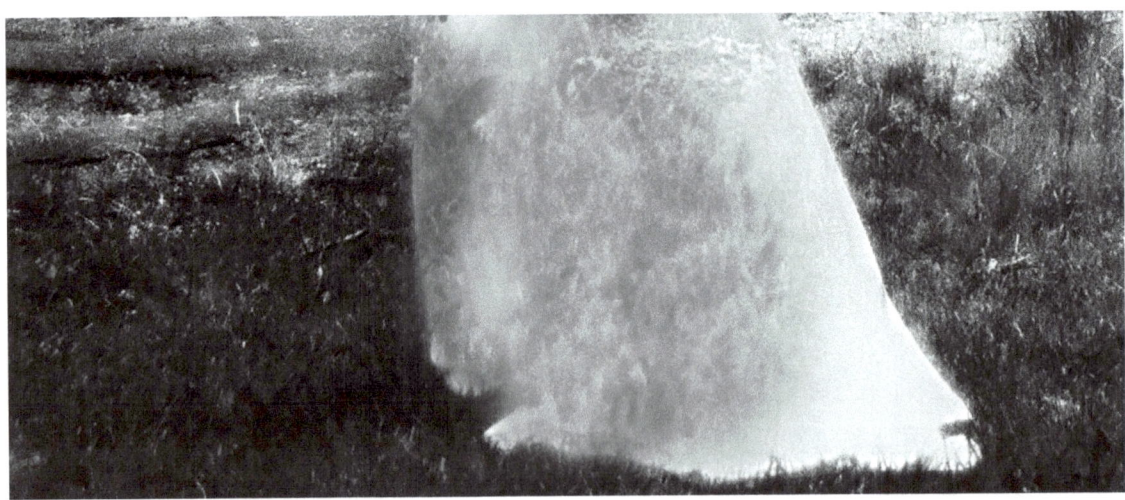

Detail: ENDLESS LOVE

Non-Evasive Love, being loved & feeling love are among my thoughts of definitions/ interpretations of this important word Love: a deep source of shared intimacy; physical yes, but also simultaneously an emotional & spiritual mutual connection which can not be replicated with another... where two could be their true selves equally / truth & commitment need not be questioned.. "love" compliments the other's life with shared laughter, understanding, fulfilled desires & intertwines with the other's needs, hopes and vision(s) naturally, during difficult times along with abundant times.

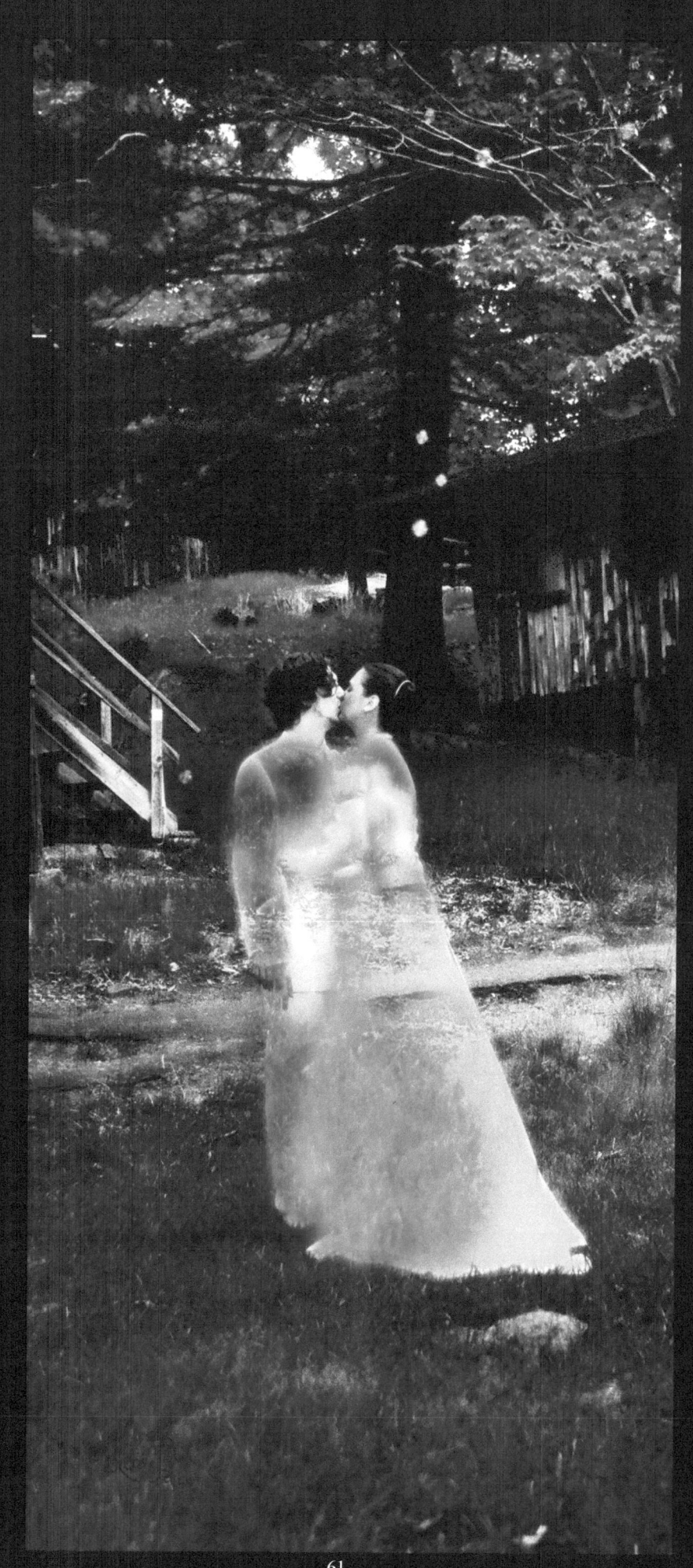

This miracle of life has surfaced for some, yes indeed without strife, to ones who have put themselves as selfless, to respect & love with open arms having value in life. Let not love be a mystery.

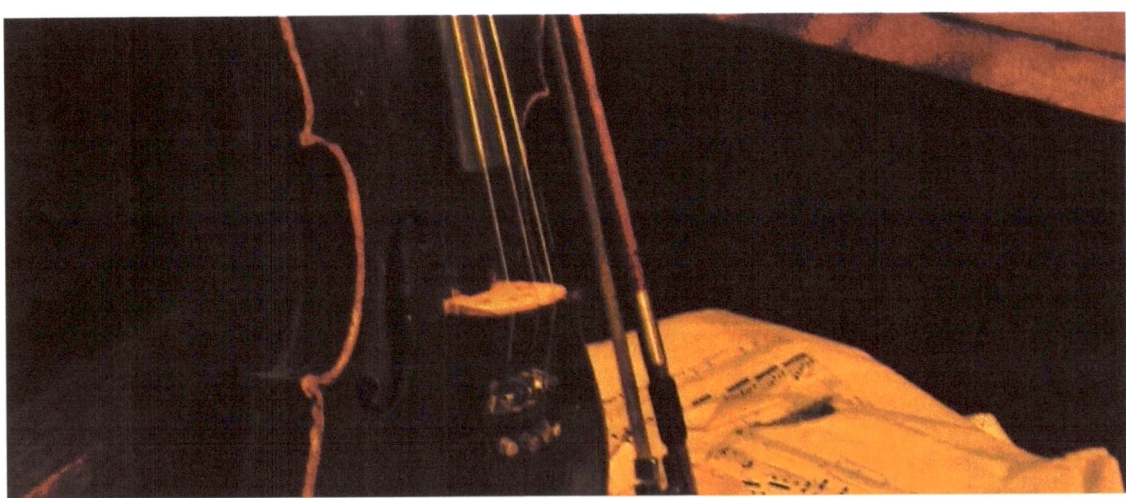

Detail: HEART STRINGS

a new skill of conversation: YOU are the One… Let's look at our meeting as a fortunate experience, to understand the people we are inside of our own protective personal personas. I hope one day to learn more about you. If we let this happen naturally and do not prejudge each other, but instead get to know each other delicately with respect, then regrets will be what's forfeited, not the future. I can see you are a very fine person with a strong compassionate selfless character. I am thankful we have met & are giving this a calm chance. Please don't shy away from interpersonal conversation. Not that I am uninterested, I too don't want to be intrusive or cross over unspoken boundaries. Take my hand S and please never hold back your heart from speaking with mine.

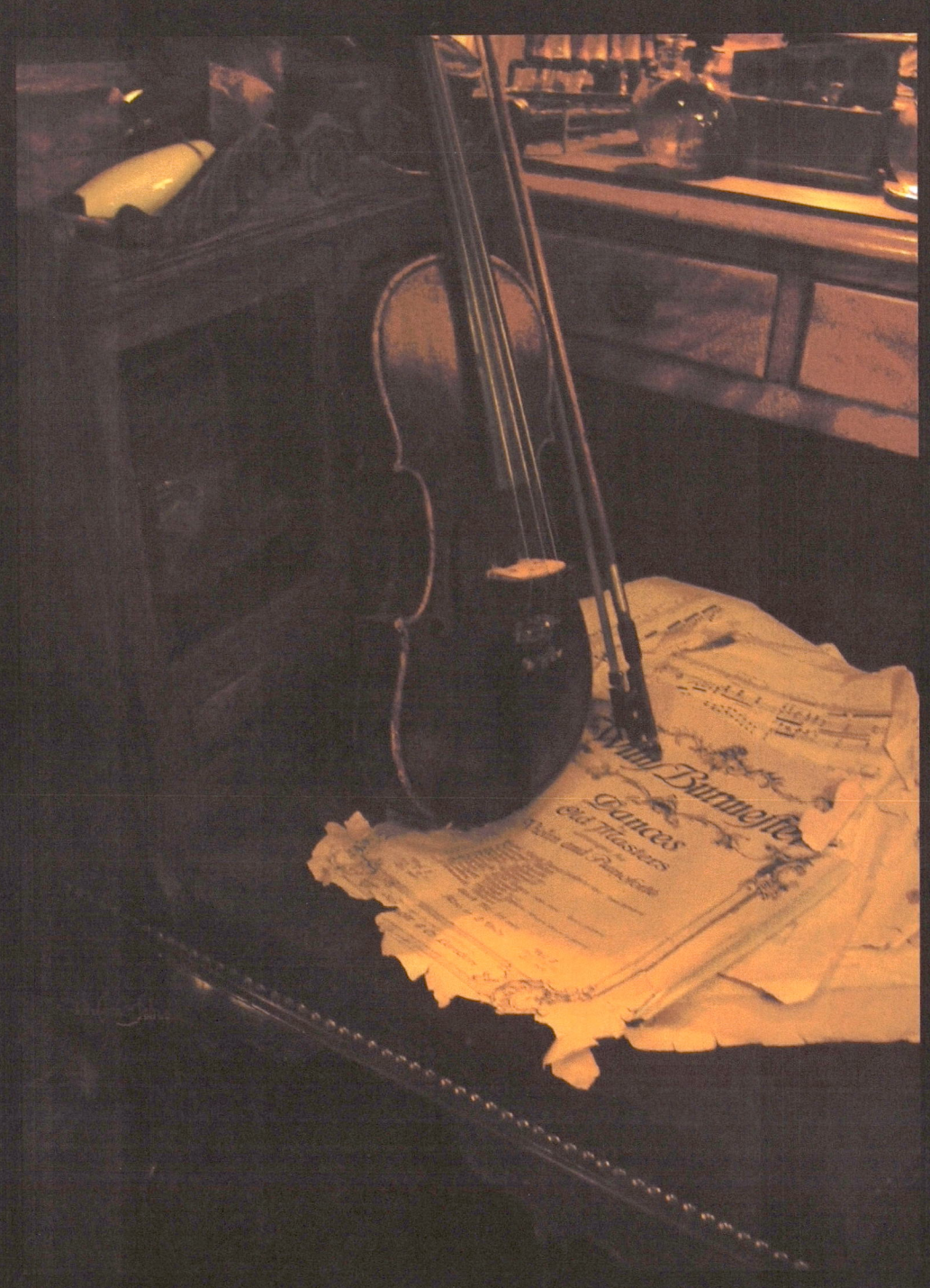

gary a., archiprete brothers, nataline a., robin a., alan a., sheree a.,alex b., raj b., glenn b., rich b., maryann b.
steve b., genny b., laurie&jihan b., melissa b., aj c., anne&larry c., wendy&frank c., john c., wolf c., laurie c.
ann&barry&winston c., francesco d., fran d., arnold d., pat&gabby d., roger d., megan d., diane d., jan d.
cornelius&ida d., michelle e., dana&zoe f., paul f., david f., harrison f., issac g., maria g., david&lynette g.
juli g., shiggaion g., laurence g., staci&keith g., myrna g., oriana g., mariel g., melanie g., helene&ken g.
gary h., sue&yaacov h., leona&clair h., betty&lens h., kim h., bobie h., roberta h., barry h., vince i.
connie&dana&jd j., maryAnn k., ruth k., christine&max k., brian k., missy&jay k., judy k., danielle k.
malinda i., marlene k., daile k., caroline&richard l. liz&johnston&laura l., becky l.
stacia&robert l., alex&jen l, jessie&freddie l. lynn l. veronica l.
evan l., magnus l., cindy l. paloma l.
lotfai&princess, lynn h., marcCat
magielnicki family, louise h., barb&ron m.
maasch family, merrill family
katie&bret m., joan&len&holland m.
essie m., sherry m., candyce m.
jacky m., "2 marias", mike m.
dom m., debra m., bob m.
merrilee m., jerry m.

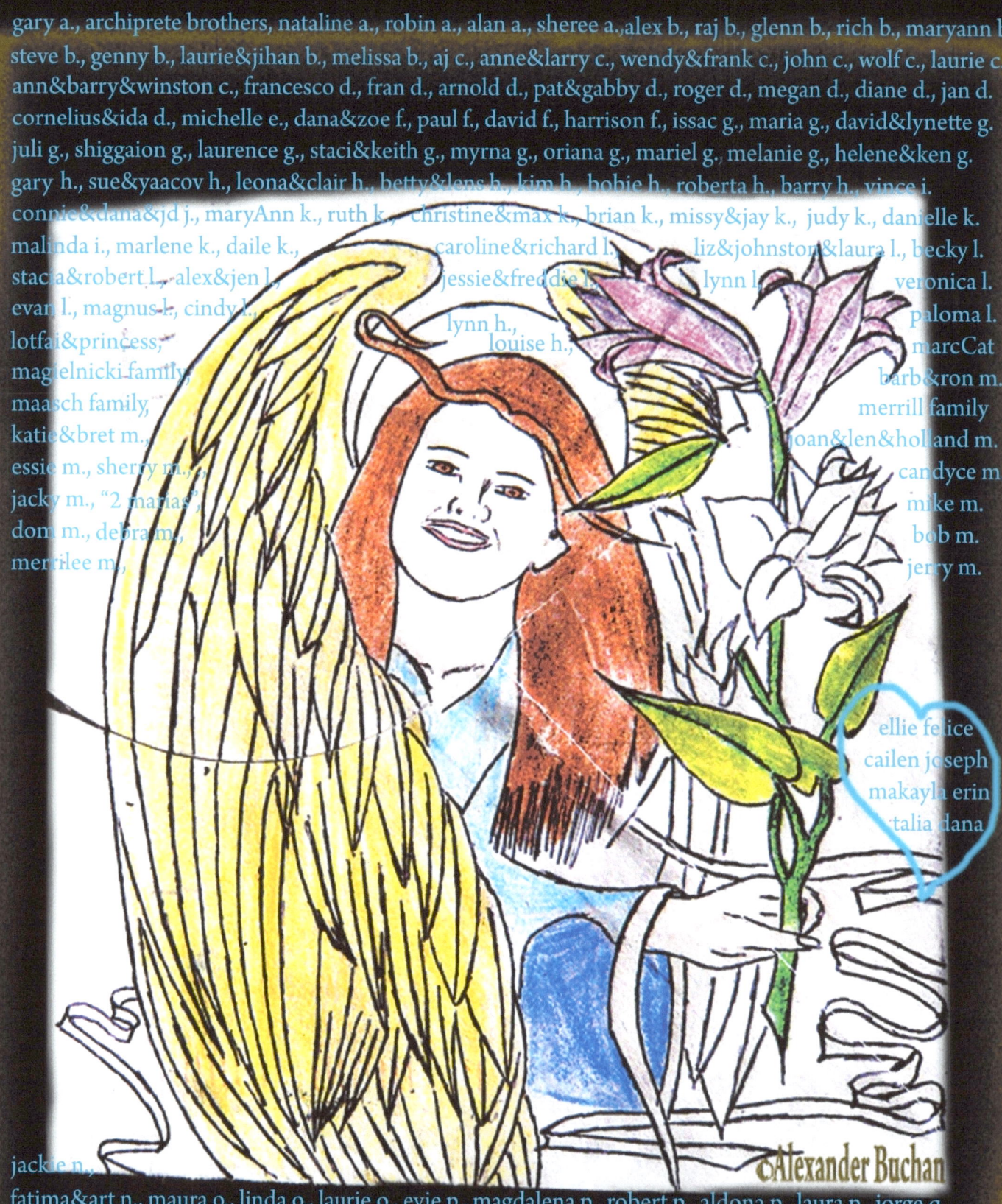

ellie felice
cailen joseph
makayla erin
talia dana

©Alexander Buchan

jackie n.,
fatima&art n., maura o., linda o., laurie o., evie p., magdalena p., robert p., aldona p., laura p., jorge q.
carol r., reid family, helen&don r., sheryl r., tone r., virginia r, rolfe r., marsha&dick r., chris&lisa r.
kumar r., jules&martin r., millie r., carol s., bill s., cynthia&harold s., jackee&robert s., cynthia s., kim s.
simon family, melinda s., pastor bill s., andy s&janet w., jodi&david s., sharon s., ekaterine s., marjana s.
turner family, rita t., iveth&laura t., steve s., cassie t., mariejo t., davida t., amiee v., rajesh v., emilija v.
adam w., winnie w., john&laura w., marianne w., marthanna y., richard z., stephie z.

I've visited a place I've never been   -Stephen John Booker

1.
I've visited a place I've never been
In no geography book this location
but found in a sleep known as dream,
Revealed only in hidden sensation.

Awakened In conscious mind
A mist of lingering scent,
A passionate yearning to find.......
to bring alive that dreamed event

Left with mind on such a high
so often we must concede,
It matters not how hard we try
this path, conscious life will not lead

So many dreams from our life,
where experience guides our way
When in life we've faced our strife
sub conscious mind has much to say

2.
I've visited a place I've never been
In no geography book this location
A place of destiny in repeated dream
Sustained in mind by fascination

Some will say life's a miracle
yet see the suffering and the pain,
describe heartache as an obstacle
Some we know are shallow and vain

In my life is an anomaly here?
For if I'm asleep do I have to fear
that some time now I will awaken
to find the love I feel, is mistaken

From experience it will often be
that dreams will differ from reality
Yet more we know, yet more to see
Can we ever reach life's tranquility?

3.
I've visited a place I've never been
In no geography book this location
where I've been and what I've seen
have such love can it be a dream?

With life experience as my guide
A passion to succeed at my side
To be awake in such emotional state,
does surely reflect that life is great

Can this be reality and not a dream?
That lingering scents ecstatic taint,
On clothes and mind, 'what does it mean'?
A strength of feeling without restraint?

Hundreds of people pass my gaze,
Voices and sounds are all around
But my eyes they will all erase
For in my senses only you abound

A feeling of but one desire
Overwhelming in its power
To keep you happy I aspire
To cherish as a delicate flower

Of few words spoken I do concede
I can better communicate in a deed
My knowledge and learning practically taught
My aspiring love, now in my thought

4.
I've visited a place I've never been
In no geography book this location
And from this place I have one view,
a vision that's the loveliness of you...

AUTHOR'S PERSONAL ANALYSIS & EXPLANATION

Ps:… the following is a 'personal' reflective study with created hypothesis I once did to remind me of my intellectual capabilities while establishing needed calm & actual personal growth:

….<u>FRAGMENTS LINKED, REFLECTION to REBIRTH, I WILL</u>… <u>TREASURE LIFE</u>

MARRIAGE to DIVORCE
- Self
- Happiness
- Commitment
- Innocence
- Reality
- Agony
- Disbelief
- Mistrust
- Descent/separation
- Withdrawal
- Escape
- Woe
- Reflection/Rebirth

LOVE to REJECTION
- Disregard
- Surprise
- Denial
- Confusion
- Try to please/justify
- Dismay
- Obedience
- Alarm/abuse
- Hope/rationalize
- Disappointment
- Mistrust
- Heartache
- Acceptance/Truth

ACCEPTANCE V.S. TRUTH
- Acceptance= Complacency- Separate lives- Delay of inevitable separation
  - In a 2 sided lie with separate lives without conclusive truth
  - Un-fulfillment of basic needs for total loving, peace and understanding
  - Future years of uncertainty
- Truth= Separation- Loneliness- Anger- Possible healing
  - Love from understanding truth; back to false hope stage if foundations remain
  - Alternate replacement
  - Acknowledgement of failure of relationship; no fault blamed on either side

REASONS for non-commitment:
- Initial:
  - Non fulfillment of ideals
  - Superiority positioning
  - Discovery of stress from relationship
- Delayed:
  - Wanted change in direction of life's course
  - Outside alternative
  - Freedom of lifestyle & alternative choices not able in current relationship
  - New person of interest

PROTECTION from __ *   (*'temporary suicide', or for others can use own personal fears*):
- Causality:
  - Foundations regarded as false; affect: in emotional level
  - Physical paralysis from outside factors; affect: in physical level
  - Decision making is reactionary; based on uncertain outcomes
    - Identify:
      - Certain outcomes= _____
      - Uncertain outcomes= _____
    - Variables due to:
      - Incoming factors= _____
      - Outgoing factors= _____

Ability to Cope:
    Emotionally:
        Ability to handle embarrassment, humiliation & verbal abuse
    Physically:
        Ability to maintain income, work load, mandated paperwork & responsibilities
Find Future Vision:
    Work on clearing path for vision by doing above coping
    Work on building a realistic and tangible road to vision's materialization
    Create applicative resumes, contact & follow up with potential employers
    See possibilities without heaviness, envision happiness
    Use relativity to see it has been & is being done by others as a part of life

Never forget the "5 Year Plan/5 Immediate Truths" I created to give me strength & legitimate hope:
    1. In 5 years the turmoil today may diminish to a bad dream.
    2. One may not know of the future's unforeseen miracles.
    3. In 5 years time there will be a new set of variables, players & circumstances without you as the center target.
    4. Think back to your personal life's time line, find strength & understanding.
    5. Love yourself unconditionally, start healing from within, God is with you.

AUTHOR'S STATEMENT OF INTENT

Sharing with you some intimate intention:

& I am aware I am far from being an authority on relationships or on life in general.

Secret thoughts to share with you, my readers; if it may help or save one life it is worth my risk of self embarrassment and chance of ridicule, so here goes>>>This is how I was able to put into perspective my 'life' when darkness & private tears were overwhelming to me: ...links back to the title of this book, a title which now YOU can change to reflect where YOU are now in life. Also, please use the images to create your own personalized journal of reflection & investigation>> yes life is a treasure, never forget the person YOU are, no one & nothing from the outside should define your worth. Life is relevant yet, your path is a lifetime directly belonging to YOU. Freedom of the heart and spirit cannot be tamed nor should it be. When/or if you feel critical of yourself, doubt your reality, or have lost all hope of a meaningful existence, please REMEMBER my '5 Year Plan' of projection to help you not hurt yourself or those who love you. And also, please remember that you are Not alone. Isolation is a universal detriment of being human, although we all belong to humanity & to this international world of 'community'. When a person is weakened & their motivation has expired this is when we must open our hearts and reach out to others who ALSO feel the same exact loss of hope... A smile, a nice note or anonymous gift of love will save a life from the downward spiral, and will truly give needed oxygen to your personal flame. When we are at our weakest, we MUST realize that many others also have isolation and despair, We can help each other because we understand their sorrow, we know the hidden secrets of the deep feelings of despair & death, AND our innermost wish may also be to put life in perspective as to regain hope and assistance for rebirth. Hey! > rebirth is not actually starting over, rather it is our true self resurfacing!!!
Much Love, denise xoxoxo

my psychobabble to you with a hug from my heart   -denise felice

YOUR perspective on interpersonal dynamics molds your individuality. Confidence in life begins with choices and also with trusting ourselves to know that personal direction is always a choice...

Necessity is the mother of re-invention. Can you open up to yourself & acknowledge who you are?> wants, desires, needed forgiveness, secrets?

Happiness is uncontrived & can be reached when our natural instinctual need to be oneself is accepted in our functional environment.

Quest first for internal happiness & contentment, then the physical environment of happiness has a better chance to happen. Don't over-think, discover what makes you unique & special... add in reflection, sensitivity & kindness to others... & of course FUN: I've found adventures can be many fold, from exploring one's mind to photographing in the highlands!

Comfort heals even for the seemingly impenetrable or needless (I am human also). Life is a journey & there will be sincere people walking the path beside us. Question only connections that are doing harm, and accept kind words from the many others as inspiration and a reflection of your own kindness...

Poor communication is only an excuse for non-caring. Everyone wants to feel cared about & understood, but then some begin to take these gifts of human connection for granted.

Prepare a strong foundation for flexibility & the ability for adaptation. Getting through rough times can create a brand new day which may only be visible & understandable once the dust has cleared.

Create good, it will multiply and return many times back to you in this close & closed circle of life!
Find special role models in life whom teach by example, to treat each & every person with dignity & omniscient understanding.

We must "trust by truth, not by words or selected actions". Wouldn't it be great if truth could prevail at all times, not trust> trust is an element that implies that one is acting in a particular way to please a person. Truth on the other hand transcends into more than mere words can describe.

A muse comes from within oneself; the muse = inner creativity... desire & also discontent / expressed via your self expression & voice via your art = YOU!

You are not insane; you are actually in the middle of insanity. The monkey in the middle never reaches the unnecessary ball which creates unnecessary want. This ball being thrown nigh close to grasp yet never attainable> thank goodness you cannot reach it, it may have exploded right in your hands and smeared over your eyes down onto your heart.

Man's interpretation of religion may form hypothesis of untruths of black & white/ good & bad. Being aware reminds me of what it is like to be a total person & to live as we have God within us.

If happiness comes naturally and is uncontrived; then is it not just an illusional state of perception when experienced? ..... or the reverse?

In Modern Society we can walk away from the hurt and not feel guilty; family members do not depend upon each other for life's sustaining tasks. Treasure the ones that treasure us, the ones that hurt us> walk away without needing to battle: they will be ok without us.

Yes, it's hard to see the big picture of life when small barriers suffocate each breath & prove happiness may be a mere concept. Yet life has to be more than this pain, I am certain.
Envision 'the BIG picture of life'; living for not just monetary values & momentary glimpses of success in competition. A broadened vision & outstretched hand will satisfy a deep need for belonging & sense of community.

we love each other : let not love be a mystery   -denise felice

Let's put up the walls not take the chance of involvement and enjoyment in life's enduring dance. We can stay safely behind in our worlds of woe, pray to fate & destiny to share with us another future blow.

For some have a life's commitment filled with devotion, nurturing & passion afire; considered not a waste of a lifetime, frivolous or supercilious desire.

We question reality, asking is it chance or fate? never appreciating ourselves or our ability to love...vanishing moments, lost connections, losing inner passion... insecurity wins at an astounding rate.

Dissatisfaction of true love, destroyed by doubt and fear of rejection, reeks havoc in our souls yet we accept as destiny; making excuses while sacrificing true happiness in search for materialistic perfection.

Painful breakdown of communication with misinterpretation of motives appear as lies, lovers can choose to rectify with heard voice, or accept with defeat & demise.

Deep rooted & grown without conscious endeavor, hurtful transference surfaces as division, yet together as one we can chose to have love flourish with sentiment & pleasure.

This discovery has begun, true intimacy more than just near, and for you & I to nurture, if we chose, without walls sharing our entire selves while letting go of expectation, judgment and fear.

To let hearts take an unbridled path nourishing love's gifts received without hesitation, realizing blindness is actual sight, mutual awareness is intrinsic/ never a creation.

The existence of a life shared in compassion & strength is cast over the edge propelled by judgmental mistrust & longing for youth. Reverence of ideal epitome creates longings not satisfaction, as we repeat the same patterns believing as truth.

Yet a lifetime of learning from our past to retreat, to wonder what's next & what we must chance, furthers stark isolation never romance. It is a game of wager, not love, again & again to role play in anticipation of ultimate defeat.

From within are cries for this solitude to not consume, for when fear pushes we surrender to self hate. Cerebral intelligence then follows as we lock our hearts in self protection with false self love to reciprocate.

All the while, as fate always knew with deep understanding why, we repeat which we have pre-wrote to create a future of misgiving, with paralysis we see yet cannot care for our spirit or appreciate the life we are living.

When one loves to love, without greed, miracles are not far behind... Life as its' self becomes a miracle when we open our eyes forgetting ourselves, our pasts, and our minds...

This miracle of life has surfaced for some, yes indeed without strife, to ones who have put themselves as selfless, to respect & love with open arms having value in life.
Let not love be a mystery.